ENGLISH in Common

with ActiveBook

Richard Acklam   Araminta Crace

Series Consultants
María Victoria Saumell and Sarah Louisa Birchley

ALWAYS LEARNING

PEARSON

ENGLISH
in Common
3
with ActiveBook

María Victoria Saumell
Sarah Louise Birchley

PEARSON

English in Common is a six-level course that helps adult and young-adult English learners develop effective communication skills that correspond to the Common European Framework of Reference for Languages (CEFR). Every level of *English in Common* is correlated to a level of the CEFR, and each lesson is formulated around a specific CAN DO objective.

English in Common 3 has twelve units. Each unit has ten pages.

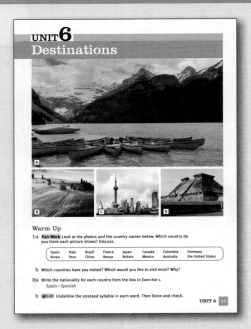

UNIT **6**
Destinations

Warm Up

1a Pair Work Look at the photos and the country names below. Which country do you think each picture shows? Discuss.

| Spain | Italy | Brazil | France | Japan | Canada | Colombia | Germany |
| Korea | Peru | China | Kenya | Britain | Australia | Mexico | the United States |

b Which countries have you visited? Which would you like to visit most? Why?

2a Write the nationality for each country from the box in Exercise 1.
Spain—Spanish

b Underline the stressed syllable in each word. Then listen and check.

UNIT 6

There are three two-page lessons in each unit.

LESSON 1 Make general predictions about the future CAN DO
GRAMMAR will: predictions

Listening

1a Pair Work Complete the map (1–7) with the words in the box. Which words can't you use?

| Lake | Beach | Island | Desert | River |
| Sea | Ocean | Forest | Mountain | |

b Listen and check your answers.

2a Pair Work Decide on the correct information about New Zealand.
1. The population is *4 million/40 million*.
2. The number of sheep is *4 million/40 million*.
3. The capital of New Zealand is *Auckland/Wellington*.
4. The national symbol is a *kiwi bird/kiwi fruit*.

For years, many people thought that New Zealand was famous for sheep, rugby, and . . . more sheep. But suddenly these islands have a new image. They are now one of the most fashionable tourist destinations in the world. And it's all because of a movie, or actually three movies. *The Lord of the Rings* series was filmed in New Zealand, and it's a wonderful ad for the country. People now want to visit New Zealand to see the places in the movies. Tourism in New Zealand is doing very well—that's the LOTR effect. Some tourists come just to see the movie locations. For example, there's a beautiful place called Matamata just south of Auckland, and 250 tourists come here every day. They pay 30 dollars each to see the remains of Hobbiton village from the first *The Lord of the Rings* movie.

it won't stop there. Some peopl that New Zealand will soon have 3 million tourists a year. But the some questions about all this su Will tourism change the natura of the landscape? Will it affect wildlife? And will tourists still w to visit New Zealand if these th happen?

Mount Ngauruhoe was "Mount Doom" in LOTR

American English	British English
movie	film
ad	advert

Active Grammar

Use *will* (+ verb) to make predictions about the future. The negative of *will* is *won't* (*will not*).

1. The number of tourists _____ in the near future.
2. It _____ (not stop) there.
3. _____ tourism _____ (change) the beauty of the landscape?

See Reference page 66

LESSON 2 Give explanations for choices CAN DO
GRAMMAR adverbs: too, too much/many, enough

Listening

1a Look at the photo and read the TV guide excerpt. What is the show *Frontier House* about?

Frontier House
Channel 4 • 7:30 P.M.

Can modern people cope with 19ᵗʰ-century life? The Clune family from California decided to find out. For six months the parents and their four children lived like Americans in the Wild West over 100 years ago.

What did they find difficult? How did the experience change them? Watch *Frontier House* and find out how modern people cope with old-fashioned life.

An American frontier family in the 1800s

b Pair Work Try to predict what each family member will find difficult about being in *Frontier House*.

Father	
Mother	
Teenage girls	
Boys (ages nine and eleven)	

2a Listen to two people talking about *Frontier House* and check if your predictions in Exercise 1b were correct.

b Listen again and circle the correct choice.
1. They lived in the style of people in about *1818/1880*.
2. The nearest store was *six/sixteen* kilometers away.
3. The father became *thinner/ill*.
4. The mother *missed/didn't miss* her make-up.
5. At first, the children *liked/didn't like* having so much to do.
6. The girls missed *shopping/TV* the most.
7. At the end of the experience, Tracy said her clothes were *more/less* important to her.

3 What do you think happened when they went home? Listen and see if you were right.

4 Group Work Discuss.
1. Would you like to be in a TV show like *Frontier House*? Why or why not?
2. Which country would you like to live in for six months, (a) now? (b) 100 years ago? Give your reasons.

60

Grammar | adverbs: too, too much/many, enough

5a Look at the two sentences. Is the meaning the same or different?
He was *too weak*. He *wasn't strong enough*.

b Match the rules and the examples in the Active Grammar box.

Active Grammar

____ 1. Use *too* with adjectives and adverbs.
____ 2. Use *too much* with non-count nouns.
____ 3. Use *too many* with count nouns.
____ 4. Use *(not) enough* after adjectives and adverbs.
____ 5. Use *(not) enough* before nouns.

a. They weren't warm enough.
b. I'm too tired to do any more work today.
c. I had too much time and nothing to do.
d. They often didn't have enough food.
e. There were too many things to do.

See Reference page 66

6 Complete these sentences using the words in parentheses and *enough*, *too*, *too much*, or *too many*.
Ex: My coat isn't *warm enough* for me. (warm)
1. I'm very tired. I went to bed _____ last night. (late)
2. I'm very busy today. I have _____ to do. (things)
3. I didn't have _____ to do my homework yesterday. (time)

that _____ crowded today.
money, so we _____ on vacation this year.
whole country in two weeks. It's too big.
ur driving test. I'm sure you _____.
look very good. Do you think it _____?
y dog. He _____ you.

ge 131 and answer the questions with a partner.

LESSON 3 Describe a favorite place CAN DO
GRAMMAR uses of like

Reading

1 Pair Work What do you know about Nelson Mandela? Discuss.

He was in prison for a long time.

2 Match the pictures (A–D) on the brochure with the phrases. Then read the brochure.

____ water plants ____ plant seeds ____ harvest the fruit/vegetables ____ get rid of weeds

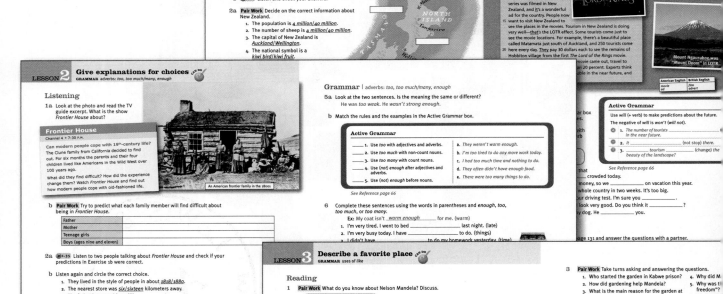

Garden of Freedom

The charity *Seeds for Africa* has started its first prison vegetable garden at Kabwe Prison in Zambia. There are 500 prisoners at Kabwe Prison, and the prison garden will give them fresh vegetables to eat. More importantly, the prison staff hope that the garden will increase the prisoners' self-esteem.¹ The Kabwe Prison garden was inspired by Nelson Mandela,

"A garden was one of the few things in prison that I could control. It gave me the simple but important satisfaction of planting a seed, watching it grow, watering it, and then harvesting it. It was a small taste of freedom. In some ways, I saw the garden as being like my life. A leader must also look after his garden; he, too, plants seeds and then watches,

3 Pair Work Take turns asking and answering the questions.
1. Who started the garden in Kabwe prison?
2. How did gardening help Mandela?
3. What is the main reason for the garden at Kabwe prison?
4. Why did M
5. Why was t freedom"?
6. What does

Grammar | uses of like

4a Match the questions and the answers in the Active Grammar box.

Active Grammar

____ 1. What *do you like* to do in your free time?
____ 2. What *would you like* to do today?
____ 3. What *is* your garden *like*?
____ 4. What *does* your garden *look like*?

a. I'd lik
b. I like
c. It's ve
d. It's ve

See Reference page 66

b Match the definitions with the different uses of *like*.
____ 1. want or want to do
____ 2. enjoy
____ 3. appearance
____ 4. character or characteristics

a. be like
b. like
c. look like
d. would like

Pronunciation | reductions

5 Listen to sentences 1–2 in the Active Grammar box. How *you* and *would you* pronounced?

6 Pair Work Write questions using *like*, *look like*, *would like* to, o ask and answer the questions.
Ex: Do you enjoy gardening? *Do you like gardening?*
1. Tell me about your best friend. _____

A two-page Unit Wrap Up and a Reference page end each unit.

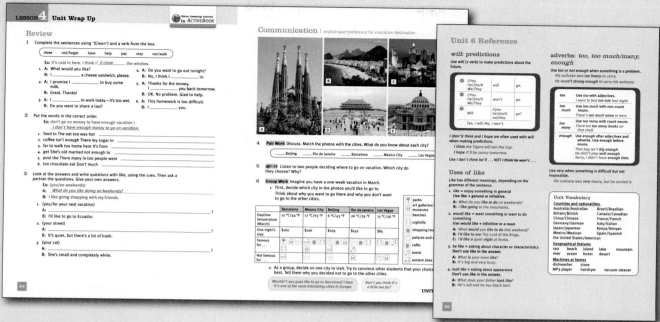

Back of Student Book

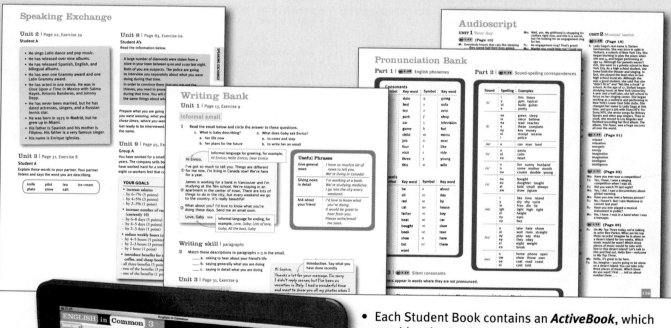

- Each Student Book contains an **ActiveBook,** which provides the Student Book in digital format. *ActiveBook* also includes the complete Audio Program and Extra Listening activities.

- An optional **MyLab** provides students with the opportunity for extra practice anytime, anywhere.

- The Teacher's Resource Book contains teaching notes, photocopiable extension activities, and an **ActiveTeach,** which provides a digital Student Book enhanced by interactive whiteboard software. *ActiveTeach* also includes the videos and video activities, as well as the complete Test Bank.

Contents

READING/WRITING	LISTENING	COMMUNICATION/ PRONUNCIATION
Reading texts: • personality profiles • an article about Tiffany's **Writing tasks:** • write about your typical Saturday • write an email to a friend	**Listening tasks:** • recognize subject matter • identify key information	**Communication:** talk about your learning needs and abilities **Pronunciation:** vowel sounds /u/, /ə/, /ʌ/
Reading texts: • an article about Lady Gaga • an article about music and the brain • biographies of three Latin pop singers **Writing task:** write a short biography of a partner	**Listening tasks:** • discern details • identify main ideas	**Communication:** explain why you like a piece of music **Pronunciation:** past-tense -ed endings
Reading texts: • an article about a celebrity chef • an email invitation • a report on a study about how we rate food **Writing task:** write an email invitation	**Listening tasks:** • recognize main ideas • determine actions and plans • identify foods	**Communication:** contribute to a simple discussion **Pronunciation:** silent letters
Reading texts: • an article about extreme adventurers • an article about England **Writing task:** write a thank you note	**Listening tasks:** • confirm a prediction • identify key information • discern main ideas • recognize decisions	**Communication:** agree on choices with a partner **Pronunciation:** sentence stress
Reading texts: • a profile of a young Chinese woman • an online personal profile **Writing task:** write a personal profile	**Listening tasks:** • recognize main ideas • identify importance of biographical details	**Communication:** make a simple informal presentation **Pronunciation:** *used to/didn't use to*
Reading texts: • an article about New Zealand tourism • a brochure about a prison garden program **Writing task:** write a description of your favorite place	**Listening tasks:** • label a map • understand important details • check predictions • identify a decision	**Communication:** explain your preference for a vacation destination **Pronunciation:** reductions
Reading texts: • an article about an actress and body image • a guide to determining personality type • a quiz about stress **Writing task:** letters requesting and giving advice	**Listening tasks:** • match descriptions to pictures • recognize main ideas • identify "problems"	**Communication:** understand and talk about a magazine quiz **Pronunciation:** choice questions with *or*
Reading texts: • an article with tips on "slowing down" • a letter describing "speed dating" • jokes **Writing task:** write a story	**Listening tasks:** • understand the gist • discern details	**Communication:** talk for an extended period on a familiar topic **Pronunciation:** rising and falling intonation in questions
Reading texts: • advice for a successful job interview • an article about Mark Zuckerberg **Writing task:** write a "news article"	**Listening tasks:** • distinguish between true and false information • understand the gist and analyze details	**Communication:** take part in a simple negotiation **Pronunciation:** word stress
Reading texts: • an article about children raised by wild animals • opinions on the pros and cons of zoos • information on animal protection organizations **Writing task:** write opinions on issues	**Listening tasks:** • distinguish between true and false information • identify key words • identify sounds	**Communication:** participate in making a group decision **Pronunciation:** sentence stress
Reading texts: • an excerpt from a travel diary • advice for business travelers **Writing tasks:** • explain your choice in a travel companion • write about a place you have traveled to	**Listening tasks:** • determine differences • identify questions • determine important details • identify key travel-related words	**Communication:** achieve your goals in a typical travel conversation **Pronunciation:** past perfect contractions
Reading texts: • results of a survey about cheating • an article about a lawsuit over a baseball **Writing task:** write a formal letter	**Listening tasks:** • understand the main ideas • verify answers • determine key points	**Communication:** make a simple complaint in a store/restaurant **Pronunciation:** *both, either,* and *neither*

How much do you know . . . ?

1 Do you know these grammar terms? Complete the chart with the <u>underlined</u> words from sentences below.

1. She is <u>a</u> doctor.
2. <u>They</u> are very generous.
3. This book is <u>yours</u>.
4. <u>Does</u> she eat meat?
5. You <u>can</u> smoke outside.
6. Keith <u>has written</u> four novels.
7. How much <u>water</u> do you drink every day?
8. Could you give this <u>pen</u> to him?
9. This watch is <u>cheaper</u> than the last one.
10. <u>He's</u> very late.

a. pronoun	*They* (sentence 2)
b. count noun	
c. comparative	
d. possessive	
e. modal verb	
f. auxiliary verb	
g. contraction	
h. noncount noun	
i. article	
j. present perfect	

2 Do you know these parts of speech? Complete the chart with the correct words from the box.

> write   sister   carefully   give up   at   beautiful

Part of speech	Example	Part of speech	Example
1. noun		4. adjective	
2. verb	*write*	5. adverb	
3. phrasal verb		6. preposition	

3 Do you know these pronunciation terms? Look at the words in the box and answer the questions below about each word.

> sister   factory   chocolate

1. How many syllables are there?   2. Where's the main stress?

4 **Pair Work** Do you know this classroom language? Match questions to the replies below. Then practice with a partner.

1. What does "party animal" mean?
2. How do you spell "exercise"?
3. Can you say that again, please?
4. What page is that on?
5. Could you speak up a bit, please?
6. What's the answer to number 5?
7. What's our homework?
8. How do you pronounce the second word?

a. Page 13, at the end of Unit 1.
b. Do exercises 3, 4, and 5 on page 64.
c. I don't know. Ask Mario. He's good at grammar.
d. /'resɪpiz/
e. E-X-E-R-C-I-S-E
f. It's someone who likes going to parties.
g. Of course. It's really noisy in here.
h. Sure, no problem. All of it or just the last part?

Your day

Warm Up

1 Find a verb phrase in the box for each photo. Then write *D* next to the things you do every day. Write *W* next to the things you do only on weekends. Write *S* next to the things you sometimes do. Write *N* next to the things you never do.

___ sleep in	___ get up early	___ talk on the phone	___ listen to music
___ watch TV	___ go to bed late	___ check your email	___ go out for dinner
___ exercise	___ text friends	___ catch a bus/train	___ read a book
___ do nothing	___ go for a walk	___ have breakfast/lunch/dinner	

2 **Pair Work** Compare with a partner.

> *I talk on the phone every day. How about you?*

Speaking

1 Match the pictures A–C in the questionnaire below with these descriptions.

_____ 1. This person likes staying in, eating, and watching television.

_____ 2. This person likes going out, dancing, and meeting friends.

_____ 3. This person likes reading and going to museums and art galleries.

2a **Pair Work** Ask your partner the questions below and fill in the quiz for him or her.

b Compare your results. Discuss.

What kind of
person
are you?

[A]

1 Choose the *best* answer.

It's your birthday. Do you . . .
- ○ A go out with friends?
- ○ B have dinner at a restaurant with friends?
- ○ C get a DVD and a pizza?

2 It's a sunny weekend. Do you . . .
- ○ A have a picnic with family and friends?
- ○ B visit another city?
- ○ C read a magazine at home?

3 It's your lunch break at work. Do you . . .
- ○ A go to the gym?
- ○ B go to lunch with friends?
- ○ C have a sandwich at your desk?

4 It's your summer vacation. Do you . . .
- ○ A go out at night?
- ○ B go sightseeing?
- ○ C lie on the beach?

5 You go shopping on vacation. Do you buy . . .
- ○ A some clothes for the evening?
- ○ B a book about the place you're in?
- ○ C ice cream?

[B]

[C]

Mostly "A"s:

You're a real party animal and fun to be with. Don't forget to stop and rest sometimes!

Mostly "B"s:

You're a culture vulture and like learning new things. Don't forget to join the party sometimes!

Mostly "C"s:

You're a total couch potato and are usually on the sofa, doing nothing. Come on—get up and join the fun!

Reading

3 Read. Is each person a "party animal," a "culture vulture," or a "couch potato"?

<u>I don't like</u> getting up early on weekends, so I usually sleep in—sometimes until 10:30! <u>I love</u> to have a big bowl of ramen on Saturday mornings. <u>I can't stand</u> going to the gym, but I sometimes go for a walk in the afternoon. <u>I like</u> going to the park and just lying on the grass and doing nothing. <u>I'm not into</u> going out on Saturday night. I stay in and talk on the phone and watch TV.

Nobu Suzuki, Tokyo, Japan

<u>I really hate</u> doing nothing, so I get up early on Saturdays and start the day by texting friends. <u>I really like</u> to meet friends for breakfast, so I catch a bus into town. After breakfast, my friends and I sometimes go to an art gallery. <u>I'm into</u> most kinds of art, so <u>I don't mind</u> which gallery we go to. I do different things on Saturday nights. I sometimes have dinner with friends, or I stay home and read.

Lola Gutierrez, Mexico City, Mexico

American English	British English
I'm into	I'm keen on

4 **Pair Work** Ask and answer the questions.

1. What do Nobu and Lola like doing?
2. What do they dislike doing?

Grammar | likes and dislikes

5 Complete the Active Grammar box using the <u>underlined</u> phrases from Exercise 3.

Active Grammar

1. _____ to have a big bowl of ramen. 😊😊😊
2. *I really like* to meet friends. 😊😊
3. *I like* going to the park. 😊
4. _____ most kinds of art. 😊
5. _____ which gallery we go to. 😐

6. _____ going out on Saturday night. ☹️
7. *I don't like* getting up early. ☹️
8. _____ going to the gym. ☹️☹️
9. *I really hate* doing nothing. ☹️☹️

Use a noun or a gerund after these phrases. Some phrases also take the infinitive.

6 Write sentences using the cues. Don't forget to change the verb if necessary.

Ex: 😊 /watch sports on TV.   *I'm into watching sports on TV.*

1. 😊😊😊 /my job.
2. ☹️ /do crossword puzzles.
3. 😊😊 /swim in the ocean.
4. ☹️☹️ /be cold.
5. 😐 /dogs.
6. 😊 /go to the movies.
7. ☹️☹️ /talk on the phone in English.
8. 😊😊😊 /go dancing.

Speaking

7 **Group Work** Tell other students what kind of person you are and why.

I think I'm mostly a party animal, because I love going out with my friends.

8 Write a paragraph with the title "My Typical Saturday." Use the paragraphs in Exercise 3 to help you.

Listening

1a **Pair Work** Make these sentences true for you. Tell a partner.

1. I sleep a lot. 2. Sleep is a waste of time. 3. I can only sleep on a hard bed.

> *I don't sleep a lot—usually six hours a night.*

b ▶1.02 Listen to a TV show about sleep. Check (✓) the things you hear.

☐ adults ☐ cats ☐ dogs ☐ horses ☐ snakes
☐ babies ☐ children ☐ fish ☐ old people

2 Listen again and answer the questions.

1. Who sleeps about (a) seven hours _____,
   (b) seventeen hours _____, and (c) eight hours _____ every day?
2. What is strange about the way horses sleep? _____
3. What is strange about the way fish sleep? _____
4. In one year, how many hours does the average person sleep?
   a. 2,688   b. 2,860   c. 2,680
5. In one night, how many dreams does the average person have? _____

3 **Pair Work** Discuss.

1. How often do you remember your dreams?
2. How often do you have the same dream?
3. Do you have any favorite dreams?

Vocabulary | verb-noun phrases about routine actions

4a Match the questions to the answers.

1. What time do you go to bed?
2. Do you have a snack before bed?
3. How many hours do you sleep each night?
4. What time do you get up?
5. What time do you have breakfast?
6. Do you take a shower in the morning or the evening?
7. Do you ever sleep in?

a. At about 7 A.M.
b. About eight hours.
c. At about 11 P.M.
d. At about 7:30 A.M., after my shower.
e. I usually take one in the morning.
f. Yes. I always sleep in on Sundays.
g. No, I hardly ever eat before bed.

b ▶1.03 Listen and check your answers.

Grammar | simple present; adverbs of frequency

5 Look at the questions and answers in Exercise 4a again. Complete the Active Grammar box with *do*, *does*, *don't*, or *doesn't*.

6 Circle the correct form.

A: *Do/Does* (1.) you fall asleep quickly?
B: Yes, I *do/does* (2.). I *don't/doesn't* (3.) listen to music, I just *go/goes* (4.) to sleep right away.

A: *Do/Does* (5.) you use an alarm clock?
B: No, I *do/don't* (6.). My mom *get/gets* (7.) up first, then she *wake/wakes* (8.) me.

A: *Do/Does* (9.) anyone in your family have strange sleep habits?
B: Yes, my brother *do/does* (10.). He *talk/talks* (11.) in his sleep, but he *don't/doesn't* (12.) wake up.

> **Active Grammar**
>
> Use the simple present to talk about routines (things you do every day) and habits (things you do often).
>
> ⊕ 1. *I usually go to bed about 10:30.*
> ⊖ 2. *They _____ take naps during the day.*
>   3. *He _____ sleep in during the week.*
> ❓ 4. *_____ you wake up early?*
>   5. *_____ she usually have a snack before bed?*
>
> **Adverbs of frequency**
>
> *never, hardly ever, sometimes, often, usually, always*
> *0%* ————————————————➤ *100%*

See Reference page 16

Pronunciation | vowel sounds /u/ and /ʌ/

7a Match the vowel sounds to the underlined words.

/u/ /ʌ/

_____ 1. A: Do you take a nap during the day?
_____ 2. B: Yes, I do.
_____ 3. A: Does Jane get up early?
_____ 4. B: Yes, she does.

b ▶1.04 Listen and check. Practice with a partner.

Speaking

8 **Pair Work** Ask and answer the questions in Exercise 4a and Exercise 6.

> *What time do you go to bed?*   *I usually go to bed at about midnight.*

Reading

1 **Pair Work** Discuss.

   1. What do you see in the photos?

   2. What do you think this article will be about?

THE LITTLE BLUE BOX

Are you hoping someone will give you a little blue box from Tiffany's on your birthday? Do you know the history of that little blue box? It was in 1837 that 25-year-old Charles Lewis Tiffany opened Tiffany and Company in New York City. The store soon became famous for beautifully designed jewelry and large, expensive gems—and the "Tiffany Blue" box, which Tiffany introduced the year he opened the store.

 The New York City store on Fifth Avenue is still important, and it brings in almost 10 percent of Tiffany's sales. But Tiffany now has 220 stores across the Americas, Asia, and Europe and is opening new stores in China and India.

People all over the world know Tiffany Blue. The color is so important to Tiffany that the company has copyrighted it. No other store can use this shade of blue.

Tiffany is still selling many of its timeless designs. But modern artists such as Paloma Picasso and Frank Gehry are also designing jewelry for Tiffany. Whether classic or modern, though, the jewelry will always come in the little blue box.

2 Read the article and take turns asking and answering the questions.

   1. How old was Charles Tiffany when he opened the store?

   2. What year did he introduce the little blue box?

   3. Where does Tiffany have stores?

   4. What kind of jewelry does Tiffany sell?

   5. Why is Tiffany the only store that can use Tiffany Blue?

3 **Pair Work** Discuss.

   1. Would you like to shop at Tiffany? Why or why not?

   2. What are your favorite stores to shop at? Why?

Listening

4a ▶1.05 Listen to a reporter outside Tiffany's. Complete the chart.

Where are you from?	What are you doing in New York?	What are you doing at Tiffany's?
Person 1:	*visiting her sister*	
Person 2:		*looking for a ring*
Person 3:	*shopping*	

  b **Pair Work** Compare your answers with a partner.

Grammar | present continuous

5 Read the Active Grammar box. How is the present continuous used in each sentence 1–6? Write *a* or *b*.

6 Circle the correct choices.

1. I *take/'m taking* a Spanish class this year. It *starts/is starting* at 7:30 on Mondays.

2. What *do you do/are you doing* these days? *Do you still study English/Are you still studying English?*

3. Yuko *doesn't eat/isn't eating* meat. She *doesn't like/isn't liking* it.

4. What *do you usually do/are you usually doing* during summer vacation?

5. They *often go/'re often going* to Costa Rica with friends.

7 ▶1.06 Listen. What is happening? Answer in complete sentences. Begin like this: *Someone is . . .*

8 **SPEAKING EXCHANGE**

Student A: Look at the picture on the right.
Student B: Look at the picture on page 128.
Find five more differences.

> *Is the man buying a DVD?*

> *No, he isn't. He's buying a book.*

Writing

9 Read the email in the Writing bank on page 133. Do the exercises.

10 Write an email to a friend you haven't talked to in a while. Tell him or her about your life right now.

> Hi Angela,
> How are you? I have so much to tell you . . .

Active Grammar

Use the present continuous for:

a. actions happening at this moment

b. temporary actions happening "around now" but not at this moment

➕	_____ 1. *I'm studying engineering.*
	_____ 2. *My girlfriend is shopping for clothes.*
➖	_____ 3. *I'm not talking on the phone.*
	_____ 4. *We're not exercising enough.*
❓	_____ 5. *Are you working in the city this week?*
	_____ 6. *What are you eating?*

Use the simple present (NOT the present continuous) with stative verbs (**Ex:** *be, know, like, love,* etc.).

See Reference page 16

Review

1 Complete the conversations with the correct form of the simple present. Then practice with a partner.

Ex: **A:** _Do you get up_____ (you/get up) early?

B: Yes, I do. On weekdays _____ (1. I/get up) at about 6:30.

_____ (2. I/go to bed) early, too.

A: _____ (3. you/go to bed) before ten o'clock?

B: No, I don't, but _____ (4. I/fall asleep) in front of the TV sometimes.

A: My brother is a very good swimmer.

B: _____ (5. he/swim) a lot?

A: Yes, he does. _____ (6. He/get up) very early and

_____ (7. swim) for two hours before breakfast. Then

_____ (8. he/go) back to the pool after work.

B: _____ (9. he/go) out with his friends much?

A: Only on weekends. _____ (10. He/not/go) out during the week at all.

2 Complete the conversations using the present continuous form of the verbs in the box.

> ~~do~~   have   sit   check   watch   go   listen

Ex: **A:** What _are you doing_____ (you) right now?

B: I _____ (1.) on a bus with some friends. We _____ (2.) downtown. What about you?

A: I _____ (3.) lunch with my family.

B: _____ (4. Jack) TV?

A: No, he isn't. He _____ (5.) to music and _____ (6.) his email.

3 Circle the correct choice to complete each sentence.

Ex: I (usually go/am usually going) to work by car.

1. Listen to that man. What language _does he speak/is he speaking_?
2. It _doesn't rain/isn't raining_ much in the summer here.
3. You _work/'re working_ very hard today.
4. _Do you prefer/Are you preferring_ tea or coffee?
5. I _stay/'m staying_ at the W Hotel in Montreal for a week.
6. Who's that woman? What _does she want/is she wanting_?

Communication | talk about your learning needs and abilities

4 Look at the Wheel of English. Match the words and phrases in the box to the pictures.

| ~~grammar~~ vocabulary reading writing listening speaking |

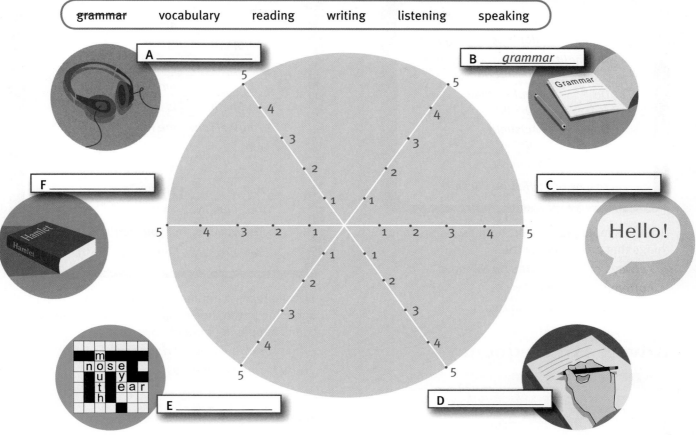

A _____

B _____*grammar*_____

F _____

C _____

Hello!

E _____

D _____

5 ▶1.07 Listen. How important is each aspect of English for Antonio? Write an **✗** at the correct place on each part of the wheel. 1 is not important; 5 is very important.

6 Listen again. How good is Antonio at each aspect of English? Make notes.

7 **Pair Work** Complete your own Wheel of English. Then explain it to your partner. Use language from the How To box.

How To:	
Talk about your learning needs and abilities	
Say what's important to you	*Grammar is (very/pretty) important to me.* *Reading is not (very) important to me.*
Say what you are good at	*I'm (very/pretty) good at listening.*

8 **Group Work** What are your strategies for learning English? Do you listen to an English language radio station? Do you keep a vocabulary notebook? Compare. Make notes about the best strategies you hear.

> *I like to write new vocabulary words on notes and put them on my refrigerator. That way I see them a couple of times a day.*

Unit 1 Reference

Simple present

⊕ ⊖	I/You/We/They	go don't go	to bed early.
	He/She/It	goes doesn't go	
❓	Do	you/we/they get up	early?
	Does	he/she/it get up	
	Yes, I do./No, I don't.		
	Yes, he does./No, he doesn't.		

Use the simple present for routines, habits, and things that are generally true.

I always call my parents on Sundays.

I often go to the movies.

He doesn't like going to bed.

Adverbs of frequency

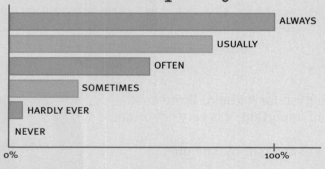

Use adverbs of frequency to say how often you do something.

I usually play tennis on Saturday.

The adverb of frequency comes after the verb *be*.

I'm never late.

The adverb of frequency comes before a main verb.

He sometimes goes out on Saturdays.

Use the affirmative with *never* and *hardly ever*, not the negative.

He hardly ever gets up early.

Present continuous

⊕	I	am	working.
	He/She/It	is	
	We/You/They	are	
⊖	I	am not	
	He/She/It	is not	
	You/We/They	are not	
❓	Am	I	sleeping in?
	Is	he/she/it	
	Are	you/we/they	
	Yes, I am./No, I'm not.		
	Yes, you are./No, you aren't.		
	Yes, he is./No, he's not (he isn't).		

Use the present continuous to talk about actions happening at the time of speaking and temporary actions happening around now.

I'm checking my email right now.

He's taking English classes this year.

Stative verbs

like	hate	prefer	understand
love	know	believe	remember
need	want		

Use the simple present (NOT the present continuous) with stative verbs.

I know how to play chess.

Unit Vocabulary

Verb-noun phrases about daily routine

read	go to the gym	talk on the phone
sleep	get up early	go out for dinner
wake up	do nothing	go to bed late
watch TV	have a snack	lie on the beach
exercise	go for a walk	meet some friends
take a nap	have a picnic	catch a bus/train
sleep in	take a shower	check your email
fall asleep	listen to music	
have breakfast/lunch/dinner		

UNIT 2
Musical tastes

A

B

C

D

Warm Up

1   What musical instruments can you see in the photos? Match the photos (A–D) to words in the box. What other instruments do you know?

| harp | violin | piano | trumpet | electric guitar |
| cello | flute | drums | saxophone | |

2   **Pair Work** Look at the types of music listed below. Try to name an artist or song for each type of music.

classical   Latin   rock   hip hop   pop   jazz

3   **Group Work** Work in small groups. Discuss.
   1. What kinds of music do you like? What kinds do you dislike?
   2. Who's your favorite singer, band, or composer?
   3. What was the last concert you went to? How was it?
   4. How often do you download music from the Internet?
   5. Do you play a musical instrument? When did you learn?

I download music from the Internet almost every week.

Really? I hardly ever do. I still buy CDs.

Reading

1 Read the article and answer the questions below.

Gaga for Lady Gaga

Before Lady Gaga's first album hit the music scene in 2008, she was an unknown 22-year-old singer-songwriter. The album, *The Fame*, brought three number-one hits, five Grammy nominations, and sudden worldwide fame for Lady Gaga. Many people were surprised at her unusual clothes (many of which she makes herself), crazy hairstyles, and wild concerts (she calls them "performance art"). But her fans love them, along with her very danceable music.

1. How old was Lady Gaga when she became famous?
2. Who writes her music?
3. Who makes a lot of her clothes?
4. What does she call her concerts?

Listening

2a ▶1.08 Listen to a short biography of Lady Gaga.

Student A: Answer the odd-numbered questions in the chart (1, 3, 5, etc.).

Student B: Answer the even-numbered questions in the chart (2, 4, 6, etc.).

1. When was she born?	
2. When did she begin performing?	
3. Where did she go to school?	
4. Was she a good student?	
5. Where did she go to college?	
6. What kind of job did she get with Sony?	
7. Where did she move in 2008?	
8. What did she finish in 2008?	

b **Pair Work** Complete the chart by taking turns asking and answering the questions you *didn't* answer. Then listen again and check your answers.

Grammar | simple past

3a Complete the Active Grammar box with the correct form of the verb in the simple past.

b Which verbs in the Active Grammar box are regular? Which are irregular?

Active Grammar

Use the simple past for completed actions in the past.

➕ 1. *She _____ her name.* (change)

➖ 2. *She _____ at school.* (fit in)

❓ 3. *Where _____ she _____ ?* (move)

See Reference page 26 and irregular verb chart on page 138

4 Complete the dialog with the simple past of the verbs in parentheses. Then practice the dialog with a partner.

    A: Where _____ (1. you/grow up)?

    B: When I _____ (2. be) very young, we _____ (3. live) in Miami. Then when I was 12, my family _____ (4. move) to Chicago. I _____ (5. not/like) it at first, but when I was a teenager, I _____ (6. love) it.

    A: _____ (7. you/go) to college when you _____ (8. graduate)?

    B: No. I _____ (9. not/go) to college until I was 22. First, I _____ (10. get) a job in a clothing store for a year and _____ (11. save) up some money. Then I _____ (12. travel). After that, I _____ (13. go) to college.

Pronunciation | past tense -ed endings

5a ▶1.09 Listen and repeat.

> worked   believed   ended   moved   wanted   loved   finished   waited   kissed

  b Put the verbs in the correct column, according to the pronunciation of -ed.

/t/	/d/	/ɪd/
worked		

Speaking

6 **Pair Work** Interview your partner about his or her life. Use the ideas below and the language in the How To box to help you. Take notes. Ask:

- when/where he or she was born
- where he or she grew up
- what he or she liked/disliked about school
- what job he or she wanted to do
- what important things happened as a teenager
- what he or she did when he or she graduated
- what important things happened after that

How To:	
Refer to times in the past	
1. Say when an action happened	• *three years ago/two months ago* • *when I finished school/when I was 15* • *in 1983/in February 1999* • *in the mid '70s/in the late '90s* • *last week/last month/last year*
2. Link an action to another action	• *after that/after finishing school* • *three years later/five days later*

Writing

7 Write a short biography of your partner. Use your notes from Exercise 6.

> Paula was born in 1990. She grew up in a small town near Bogota. She didn't like school, but she loved music . . .

Compare yourself to another person

GRAMMAR agreement: *so* and *neither*

Reading

1 **Pair Work** Think about three of your favorite songs. How does each one make you feel? Tell a partner using the adjectives in the box and your own words.

> happy   sad   relaxed
> awake   sleepy   thoughtful

> *"What a Wonderful World" made me feel relaxed and happy.*

2 Read the article. Mark the statements below true (*T*), false (*F*), or don't know (*?*).

The Mozart Effect

Music is not just entertainment. It is medicine for both the brain and the body. Don Campbell is an expert on *the Mozart effect* and the amazing power of music. He says that all kinds of music, from Mozart to jazz, from Latin to rock, can affect our learning and our health.

Many people use music to help them feel <u>relaxed</u> after a busy day at work. Music can also reduce the stress of being ill, especially by reducing pain. The director of Baltimore Hospital says that 30 minutes of classical music has the same effect as 10 milligrams of the painkiller Valium.

Campbell also says that music can help you concentrate, but you need the right kind of music for your mood. And he says you should listen for about ten minutes before you start studying. If your mind needs relaxing, or you are <u>tired</u> and you want to feel more <u>energetic</u>, you should choose the appropriate music to help you. You can use many different kinds of music to help you concentrate. Mozart's music is very popular, however, because it is very organized, and it makes your brain more alert and <u>imaginative</u>.

Music helps you study, and it can actually make you more <u>intelligent</u>. In one study, students who listened to Mozart before doing a test scored higher than those who didn't. Many studies also show that children who learn to play a musical instrument before the age of 12 can remember information better for the rest of their lives.

_____ 1. Music is good for our bodies and brains.

_____ 2. Don Campbell loves Mozart's music.

_____ 3. Many hospitals use music to help with pain.

_____ 4. Only Mozart's music helps you to study.

_____ 5. The students listened to Mozart for 15 minutes before doing the test.

_____ 6. It's a good idea for children to learn to play a musical instrument.

3 **Pair Work** Discuss.

1. What music do you listen to?   2. What effect does it have?

Vocabulary | *word families*

4a Match the underlined adjectives in the article on page 20 with the definitions below.

1. _____ = good at learning and understanding things
2. _____ = can think of new and interesting ideas
3. _____ = active and can work hard
4. _____ = calm and not worried
5. _____ = feeling that you want to rest or sleep

b Complete the table. Use a dictionary if necessary.

Adjective	Noun
relaxed	*relaxation*
energetic	
imaginative	
intelligent	

5 ▶1.10 Listen and underline the main stress in the words in the table.

1. Can you figure out any rules for word stress with nouns?
2. Which pairs of words have the same stress?
3. Which pairs have different stress?

6 Circle the correct choice to complete each sentence.

1. Latin music makes me feel *energetic/energy*.
2. I'm a very *imaginative/imagination* person.
3. I need to use my *imaginative/imagination* in my job.
4. Everyone has the *intelligent/intelligence* to learn a language.
5. I listen to music in the morning to give me *energetic/energy*.
6. Jazz makes me feel *relaxed/relaxation*.

7 **Pair Work** Use the words in Exercise 6 to make sentences about yourself.

> *Going for a run makes me feel energetic.*

Grammar | *agreement: so and neither*

8a Complete the Active Grammar box.

b **Pair Work** Cover the answers and practice the conversations from the Active Grammar box.

Speaking

9 **Pair Work** Use the phrases in the box to make sentences about music. Respond to your partner's comments.

> I have . . .   I really like . . .   I'm . . .
> I think . . .   I don't like . . .
> I'm not . . .   I sometimes go . . .

> *I really like going to see musicals.*   *So do I.*

Active Grammar

Same

1. A: *I like rock music.*   B: *So do I.*
2. A: *I'm not into him.*   B: *Neither _____ I.*
3. A: *I didn't go.*   B: *Neither _____ I.*

Different

4. A: *I usually listen to rock music.*   B: *I don't.*
5. A: *I can't play an instrument.*   B: *I _____.*
6. A: *I don't like loud music.*   B: *I _____.*

See Reference page 26

Enrique Iglesias

Alejandro Sanz

Marc Anthony

Speaking

1 **Pair Work** Discuss.

1. Do you like Latin pop? Why or why not?
2. What do you know about the singers pictured here?

2a **SPEAKING EXCHANGE** Work in groups of three. Read about one of the singers above.

Student A: Read the biographical information on page 127.
Student B: Read the biographical information on page 128.
Student C: Read the biographical information on page 131.

b Ask your partners the questions below. Then guess which singer each partner is describing.

1. What kind of music does he sing?
2. How many albums has he released?
3. Have any of his albums been in English?
4. What music awards has he won?
5. Is he married?
6. Who are his parents?

Grammar | present perfect and simple past

3 Read the examples in the Active Grammar box. Then complete the rules by writing *present perfect* or *simple past*.

Active Grammar

He grew up in Miami.
He has released over nine albums.
When was he born?
Has he been in any movies?

1. Use the _____ to talk about an action or experience at a specific time in the past.

2. Use the _____ to talk about an action or experience in the past when the time is not important or not known.

See Reference page 26

4a Complete the conversations with the present perfect or simple past.

A: _____ (1. you/ever/win) a competition?

B: Yes, I _____ (2.). I _____ (3. win) a singing competition when I was six.

A: _____ (4. you/watch) TV last night?

B: Yes, I _____ (5.). I _____ (6. see) a documentary about global warming.

A: _____ (7. you/ever/meet) a famous person?

B: No, I _____ (8.). But I _____ (9. see) Madonna in concert last year!

A: _____ (10. you/ever/play) a musical instrument in public?

B: Yes, I _____ (11.). I _____ (12. be) in a band when I was a teenager.

b ▶1.11 Listen and check your answers.

c **Pair Work** Ask and answer the questions in Exercise 4a.

Vocabulary | achievements

5a Match the verbs from A with the phrases from B.

A		B
_____ 1.	learn	a. a prize for (dancing/a sport)
_____ 2.	give	b. to speak another language
_____ 3.	start	c. a difficult test
_____ 4.	win	d. your own company
_____ 5.	pass	e. an article/a book
_____ 6.	write	f. a speech to (30 people)

b **Pair Work** Which of the above have you done/not done? Which other achievements are you most proud of in your life? Tell your partner.

> *I've played the piano in a concert.*
> *I'm really proud of that.*

Speaking

6 **Group Work** Work in groups of three. Tell your partners about a singer or musician that you like. Use the questions in Exercise 2b as a guide. Your partners guess who you are talking about.

Review

1   Complete the sentences using the simple past.

    Ex: I _learned_ to play the piano when I was a child.

    My father _taught_ me. (learn/teach)

1. He _____ his old computer and _____ a new one. (sell/buy)
2. My grandmother _____ and _____ her arm. (fall/break)
3. I was on a diet last week. I _____ only fruit and I _____ only water. (eat/drink)
4. When we _____ on vacation last year, I _____ a lot of photos. (be/take)
5. I _____ to a concert last night and _____ two really good bands. (go/see)

2   Complete the dialogs with the simple past of the verbs in the boxes. Then practice with a partner.

| ~~do~~ | say | think |
| go | meet | not/like |

| stop | like | not/like |
| hate | be | live |

A: What _did you do_ (you) last weekend?

B: On Friday night, I _____ (1.) my friend Natalia and we _____ (2.) to see a movie. I _____ (3.) it was a really good film, but Natalia _____ (4.) it. She _____ (5.) it was boring.

A: Where _____ (6. you) born?

B: In Canada. I _____ (7.) in Vancouver when I was a child.

A: _____ (8. you) it?

B: No, I _____ (9.) it. I _____ (10.) the weather because it never _____ (11.) raining!

3   Agree or disagree using *so, neither,* or short answers. Then practice with a partner.

    Ex: A: I have a headache.

        B: (agree) _So do I_.

1. **A:** I thought that coat was very expensive.
   B: (agree) _____.
2. **A:** I didn't like her last single.
   B: (disagree) _____.
3. **A:** I'm doing my homework at the moment.
   B: (agree) _____.
4. **A:** I don't go swimming much.
   B: (agree) _____.

4   Complete the sentences using the present perfect.

    Ex: Susie _has seen_ *Avatar* five times! (see)

1. I _____ of that band. (not hear)
2. _____ a marathon? (you/ever/run)
3. I _____ to Carnival in Brazil twice. (be)
4. _____ your leg? (you/ever/break)
5. She's nervous because she _____ a horse before. (not ride)
6. _____ any climbing before? (you/do)
7. I _____ all over the world. (work)
8. _____ music from the Internet? (you/ever/download)

Communication | explain why you like a piece of music

5 ▶ **1.12** You're going to hear a radio show. Listen to the introduction. What is the show about?

6a ▶ **1.13** Listen to the rest of the show and complete the chart.

Piece of music	Artist	Reason
3		
2		
1		

b Compare your answers with a partner.

7a Complete the sentences from the listening, using the phrases in the box.

> reminds me of (a time/a place/a person . . .)
> makes me (feel happy/cry/smile . . .)
> remember (listening/going/feeling . . .)

1. This music _____ great.
2. It _____ when I was in college.
3. When I first heard it, it _____ because it was so beautiful.
4. I _____ to this song when I was on vacation in Spain.

b ▶ **1.14** Listen and check your answers. Repeat the sentences.

8a Choose your top three pieces of music. Complete the chart.

Piece of music	Artist	Reason
3		
2		
1		

b **Group Work** Tell other students about your choices. Use your notes and the language from Exercise 7a.

> *It's hard, but I guess my number three choice is "I Gotta Feeling" by The Black Eyed Peas. It always makes me feel happy.*

Unit 2 Reference

Simple past

Regular verbs

- **(+)** *I played jazz music all day yesterday.*
- **(−)** *He didn't finish his exam.*
- **(?)** *Why did you wait so long?*
  Did you like the last Coldplay CD?
  Yes, I did./No, I didn't.

Irregular verbs

- **(+)** *I left Los Angeles in 1993.*
- **(−)** *They didn't come home last night.*
- **(?)** *Where did she grow up?*
  Did he go to school with you?
  Yes, he did./No, he didn't.

Use the simple past to talk about completed actions.

Use the same form for all persons (but *was/were* for the verb *be*).

Add *-ed* to regular verbs to make the past form.

Use *didn't (did not)* to make the negative.

so and *neither*

		Agree/Disagree
(+)	*I like chocolate.*	*So do I./I don't.*
	I hated swimming.	*So did I./I didn't.*
	I'm a student.	*So am I./I'm not.*
	I was into pop.	*So was I./I wasn't.*
		Agree/Disagree
(−)	*I don't watch TV.*	*Neither do I./I do.*
	I didn't go out.	*Neither did I./I did.*
	I'm not enjoying it.	*Neither am I./I am.*
	I wasn't late.	*Neither was I./I was.*

Use *so* and *neither* to say that you agree with or have the same experience as someone.

Affirmative statement: use *so* + affirmative auxiliary.

Negative statement: use *neither* + affirmative auxiliary.

Use the opposite auxiliary to say that you disagree with or have a different experience from someone.

Present perfect

Form: *have/has* + past participle

(+) **(−)**	I/You/We/They	have/haven't	won a prize.
	She/He/It	has/hasn't	
(?)	Have	I/you/we/they ever	heard this song?
	Has	he/she/it ever	
	Yes, I have./No, I haven't.		
	Yes, he has./No, he hasn't.		

Use the present perfect to talk about an action or experience in the general past—the specific time is not important or is not known.

Don't use the present perfect with past time expressions (*last night*, *two weeks ago*).

Use the simple past to talk about an action or experience at a specific time in the past.

A: *I've visited 11 countries in my life.*
B: *Have you ever been to Asia?*
A: *Yes, I have. I went to Thailand in 2001.*

Unit Vocabulary

Music

pop	jazz	hip hop
rock	Latin	composer
band	singer	classical

release an album
download music from the Internet

Word families (adjective/noun)

energetic/energy   imaginative/imagination
relaxed/relaxation   intelligent/intelligence

Achievements

give a speech   start your own company
win a prize   write an article/a book
graduate   pass a difficult test
learn to speak another language

For a list of irregular verbs, see page 140.

UNIT 3
Fine cuisine

Warm Up

1   What foods can you see in the photos?

2   Complete the sentences using the words or phrases in the box.

> cook for yourself   ~~give up eating~~   eat out   celebrity chefs   diets   vegetarian

Ex: Is there any food that you would like to _give up eating_? If so, why?

1. Have you ever been a _____? Why or why not?

2. Do you know any special _____ for people who want to lose weight fast?

3. Do you _____ very often? Do you follow recipes?

4. How often do you _____? What kind of restaurants do you like?

5. Are there any famous _____ in your country?

Tell a friend about your future plans

GRAMMAR *be going to*: future

Reading

1   Read the article and then answer the questions below.

Jamie Oliver

Food lovers everywhere love the celebrity chef Jamie Oliver. One big reason is his simple, easy, and above all tasty recipes, which he has put together in some excellent cookbooks. Good food was always very important in Jamie's family. His parents had a pub in the south-east of England, and from the age of eight he started cooking and helping the chefs.

Not long ago, he started a new project. He opened a restaurant called "15" in East London. He gave himself nine months to take a team of unemployed 16 to 24-year-olds with almost no previous cooking experience and turn them into top-class chefs. Jamie says his biggest lesson is that each individual needs a different approach. Some people learn quickly, and others need a little more time.

The project also became a TV series called *Jamie's Kitchen*, which millions of people watched. One of the real success stories was KerryAnn Dunlop. Originally, she didn't get into college, but after Jamie took her on, everything changed.

Now she runs her own section of the kitchen. "Everyone is still having a really good time. We get tired sometimes, but we have fun in the kitchen, and seeing everyone enjoying the meals we've prepared makes us all feel good." And about Jamie, she says, "He's fantastic. He's like a big brother or best friend to me now."

So what is she going to do next? "I think I'd like to work abroad. I'm going to apply for a job in a top New York restaurant."

1. Why is Jamie Oliver's food successful?
2. When did Jamie start cooking?
3. Who did Jamie employ as chefs?
4. What is surprising about KerryAnn's story?
5. How does she feel about Jamie?
6. Where would she like to work next?

2a   Match a word or phrase from **A** with a word from **B** to make phrases from the article.

A	B
a real success ___*story*___	restaurant
top-class _____	~~story~~
no previous _____	chef
open a _____	abroad
tasty _____	experience
work _____	recipe

b   **Pair Work** Take turns making sentences about Jamie or KerryAnn using the phrases above.

> *KerryAnn is one of the real success stories of the project.*

Grammar | *be going to: future*

3 ▶ 1.15 Listen to this trainee chef talk about her future plans. Then answer the questions.

   1. What are her plans for the summer?

   2. What are her plans after that?

4 Listen again and complete the sentences in the Active Grammar box.

5 Correct the sentences below. There is a word missing in each sentence.

   Ex: I ᵐgoing to be an astronaut when I grow up.

   1. They're going visit their son in Australia in the summer.

   2. What he going to do this afternoon?

   3. You going to see Sarah this weekend?

   4. We're going to tennis on Sunday morning.

   5. They not going to work abroad this summer.

   6. When are you to visit me?

   7. Ann isn't going catch the train.

6 **Pair Work** Tell your partner three things you plan to do this week—two true things and one false. Your partner must decide which is false.

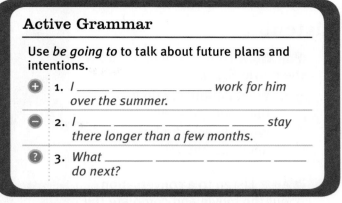

Active Grammar

Use *be going to* to talk about future plans and intentions.

➕ 1. I _____ _____ _____ work for him over the summer.

➖ 2. I _____ _____ _____ _____ stay there longer than a few months.

❓ 3. What _____ _____ _____ _____ do next?

See Reference page 36

Speaking

7a What are your plans for the next two years? Think about these areas of your life and make notes.

work	travel	hobbies and sports
home	education	friends and family

Work — change my job — earn more money

Travel — visit China — see the Great Wall

b **Pair Work** Talk about your future plans. Use the How To box to help you.

How To:

Talk about future plans	
1. Ask someone about their plans	*What are your plans for the next two years?*
2. • Describe your plans	*I'm going to learn English . . . I'm going to get a new job . . .*
• Give a time reference	*. . . this year . . . next year*
• Give a reason	*. . . because I want to work abroad. . . . to earn some money.*

LESSON 2
Write an informal invitation
GRAMMAR defining relative clauses

Listening

1 **Pair Work** Look at the photo from the movie *Big Night*. Discuss.

1. What nationality do you think the two men are?

2. What do you think the movie might be about?

2 ▶1.16 Listen to a conversation about the movie and complete the notes below.

1. *Name of film:*
   It's called <u>*Big Night*</u>.

2. *Time/place:*
   It's set in _____

   _____.

3. *Main characters:*
   It's about _____

   _____.

4. *Problem:*
   The problem is that _____

   _____.

5. *The plan:*
   The plan is that _____.

3 **Pair Work** Think of a movie you like. Make notes as in Exercise 2. Tell your partner about the movie. Use the phrases above.

> *I saw a great movie recently. It's called . . .*

Pronunciation | silent letters

4a Cross out the silent letters in the words below.

knife	island	spaghetti	comfortable	Wednesday
lamb	whistle	vegetable	chocolate	

b ▶1.17 Listen and repeat. Then check your answers.

5 ▶1.18 **Pair Work** Listen. Then read the sentences to your partner.

1. I had lamb for lunch on Wednesday.

2. Would you prefer vegetable soup or spaghetti?

3. Chocolate makes me feel calm.

4. The house on the island is very comfortable.

5. Don't forget to bring a whistle and a knife.

Grammar | relative clauses

6 Look at the examples and complete the Active Grammar box with the <u>underlined</u> words.

> *It's about two brothers <u>who</u> live in New York.*
>
> *They own a restaurant <u>that</u> isn't doing very well.*
>
> *Next door there's a restaurant <u>where</u> they serve terrible Italian food.*

7 **Pair Work** Take turns making sentences from the prompts.

> **Ex:** The news channel/I like the best/CNN.

1. Spinach/the only vegetable/I never eat.
2. The place/I feel happiest/my bedroom.
3. The town/I was born/beautiful.

Active Grammar

Relative clauses give information about people, things, and places.

They come directly after the noun.

1. Use _____ for people.

2. Use _____ for places.

3. Use _____ for things.

You can use *that* instead of *who* (informal).

See Reference page 36

> *The news channel that I like the best is CNN.*

4. My sister/the only person/looks like me.
5. The music/I listen to the most/jazz.
6. The thing/I like the most about myself/my hair.

Speaking

8 **SPEAKING EXCHANGE** Read the How To box. Then practice describing things to your partner. **Student A:** Look at page 127. **Student B:** Look at page 128.

How To:	
Describe something you don't know the name of	
Describe a count noun	*It's the thing that you use for eating cereal.* (spoon)
Describe a noncount noun	*It's the stuff that you put on pasta.* (sauce)
Describe a person	*It's the person who takes your food order.* (waiter)

Writing

9 Read the message below. Then look at the Writing bank on page 133.

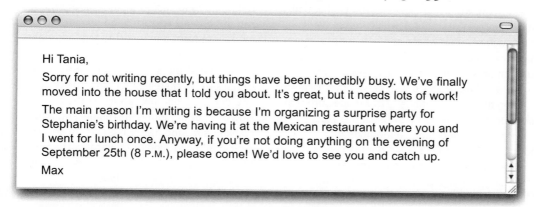

Hi Tania,

Sorry for not writing recently, but things have been incredibly busy. We've finally moved into the house that I told you about. It's great, but it needs lots of work!

The main reason I'm writing is because I'm organizing a surprise party for Stephanie's birthday. We're having it at the Mexican restaurant where you and I went for lunch once. Anyway, if you're not doing anything on the evening of September 25th (8 P.M.), please come! We'd love to see you and catch up.

Max

10 Write a short message to a friend. Give recent news and invite him or her to a party.

Make plans with a friend

Vocabulary | sensory adjectives and verbs

1 Mark the adjectives positive (+) or negative (–).

____ delicious ____ tasteless ____ tasty ____ disgusting ____ mouth-watering ____ awful

2 Match the sentences to the pictures below.

_____ 1. This **tastes** delicious! _____ 4. You **feel** hot!

_____ 2. You **look** nice! _____ 5. This doesn't **smell** great.

_____ 3. That **sounds** awful!

3 **Pair Work** Use *look*, *sound*, *smell*, *taste,* and *feel* to give your opinion about the following.

| fresh coffee | violins | being in love | diamonds |
| your shoes | old milk | chili peppers | cigarettes |

Fresh coffee smells wonderful, especially in the morning.

Reading

4 Read the article and circle the correct meaning of the <u>underlined</u> words or phrases in the text.

The Best Meal You Ever Had

For a great meal, which is more important—the food you eat or where you eat it? An article in *The Week* magazine suggests that where one eats may be more important than the food itself. Professor John Edwards and his team served chicken à la king—a chicken, mushroom, and cream sauce dish served over rice—to people in ten different <u>locations</u>.[1] They made sure that the food was always the same by using the exact same cooks, <u>ingredients</u>,[2] and cooking methods.

Among the places they served the dish were a nursing home, an army training camp, and an expensive four-star restaurant. After the meal, the researchers asked the diners to rate the food. Diners rated the taste, <u>texture</u>,[3] and <u>appearance</u>[4] of the food on a scale from one (poor) to ten (excellent).

The researchers found that diners rated the meal the lowest at the army training camp. As one soldier remarked, "It tastes awful and smells disgusting!" The dish also got low ratings at the nursing home. However, at the four-star restaurant, diners gave the chicken à la king a very high rating and said it tasted delicious! According to Edwards, "The results show that in many cases, the location is actually much more important than the food."

1. a. times   b. places
2. a. plates   b. things that go into a dish
3. how something   a. tastes   b. feels
4. how something   a. looks   b. sounds

5 Answer the questions below.

    1. Where did Edwards's team serve chicken à la king?

    2. How did they make sure it was always the same?

    3. What did the diners score the dish on?

    4. Where did the dish get the best and worst scores?

6   Pair Work   Discuss.

    1. Is the place people eat important? Why or why not?   2. Where is your favorite place to eat?

Grammar | definite plans: present continuous

7a ▶1.19 Listen to the conversation. What is the woman doing tonight?

b Listen again and complete the Active Grammar box.

8a   Pair Work   Take turns making sentences using the present continuous.

    1. I/not do/anything/tonight.

    2. Karen/go to a concert/next week.

    3. He/not go out/this weekend.

    4. We/watch TV/at home/tonight.

    5. they/spend next weekend/at the beach?

    6. I/play football/tomorrow night.

b Tell your partner about your plans.

> I'm going to the movies with my friend Tomo on Saturday.

Active Grammar

Form the present continuous with: *be* + verb + *-ing*

Use the present continuous to talk about future plans that are definite (a time and place is decided).

1. *What _____ you doing tonight?*

2. *I _____ going out for dinner with Carlos.*

3. *He _____ coming with us.*

See Reference page 36

Speaking

9 Look at the How To box. Think of other phrases to replace the underlined ones.

How To:	
Make plans	
A Check if someone is free	*What are you doing on* Friday night?
B Reply	⊕ *Nothing. Why?*
	⊖ *I'm sorry, but I'm busy. I'm seeing Jo.*
A Make a suggestion	*Why don't we try the Indian restaurant?*
B Accept/reject	⊕ *Great idea!*
	⊖ *I'm not really into Indian food.*
A Arrange to meet	*I can meet you at the restaurant at 7:00.*
B Confirm	⊕ *Great!*
	⊖ *8:00 would be better for me.*

10   Group Work   Write down your schedule for next weekend. Then make plans to do something with three different classmates. Add the plans to your schedule.

Review

1   Answer the questions below with *be going to* and the word(s) in parentheses.
Then practice with a partner.

   Ex: Have you finished the report? *(tomorrow)*   *No, I'm going to finish it tomorrow.*

   1. Have you had something to eat? (later)   _____

   2. Have you taken the dog for a walk? (after dinner)   _____

   3. Have you bought Mary a birthday present? (this weekend)   _____

   4. Have you painted the spare bedroom? (on Tuesday)   _____

2   Make questions with *be going to* for each situation.

   Ex: Your friend tells you that she is going into town.

      What _*are you going*_____ to buy?

   1. Your friend says he wants to quit smoking.   3. Your friend has bought a painting.
   When _____?   _____ put it?

   2. Tom tells you that it's Jane's birthday   4. You see a friend filling a bucket with
   next week.   hot water.
   Are _____ a gift?   Are _____ car?

3   Combine the two sentences to make one sentence with a relative clause. Use
who, *that*, or *where*. (You may sometimes need to leave out a word.)

   Ex: This is the car. I would like to buy it.   _*This is the car that I would like to buy.*_____

   1. A waiter brought our food. He was very friendly.
   The _____.

   2. This is a restaurant. John asked me to marry him here.
   This _____.

   3. A train goes to the airport. It runs every 20 minutes.
   The _____.

   4. This is the corner. The accident happened here.
   This _____.

4   Look at Carla's schedule. Write complete sentences about her plans.

   1. _*She's going to the dentist on Monday.*_

Monday		2. _____
DAY OFF!	11 A.M. dentist	3. _____
	2 P.M. lunch with Jenny	4. _____
	6:30 P.M. Italian class	5. _____
Tuesday		6. _____
10 A.M. presentation to sales reps		7. _____
3 P.M. meeting with marketing director		8. _____
6 P.M. call US office		
8 P.M. movie with Nathan		

Communication | contribute to a simple discussion

5 **Group Work** Tell other students about one of your favorite restaurants. Describe:

- the kind and quality of food
- the size of the restaurant
- the service
- the prices
- the kind of people who go there
- the general atmosphere

6 ▶1.20 Listen to a man talking about his plans. Complete the menu.

THE *art* RESTAURANT

Appetizers

Goat cheese salad

(1.) _____

Garlic mushrooms

Main courses

Vegetarian pasta

(2.) _____

Roast chicken and vegetables

Desserts

Apple pie with ice cream

(3.) _____

Cheesecake

7a **Group Work** You're going to open a new restaurant. Discuss the following:

- the location
- the prices
- the name of the restaurant
- any special features
- what kind of music (if any)
- the decoration
- menu items

b Tell other groups your ideas. Vote for the group with the best chance of success.

be going to: future

Use *be going to* to talk about something you intend or plan to do (you have already decided to do it).

A: *Are you going to see Sally this week?*

B: *I don't know. I'm going to call her this evening.*

➕	I	am	going to	see Maria on Friday.
	He/She/It	is		
	We/You/They	are		
➖	I	am	not going to	
	He/She/It	is		
	You/We/They	are		
❓	Am	I	going to	see her?
	Is	he/she/it		
	Are	we/you/they		
	Yes, I am./No, I'm not.			

Future time expressions are often used with *be going to* (*this afternoon, tonight, tomorrow, next week*, etc.).

Defining relative clauses

Defining relative clauses give us more information about a noun.

They answer the questions: *Which person? Which thing? Which place?*

Relative clauses come immediately after the noun in the main clause.

Use *who* to talk about people, *that* to talk about things, and *where* to talk about places.

*This is **the book that** you want.*
*She's **the teacher who** lives in my building.*
*That's **the store where** I bought these shoes.*

That can be used instead of *who*.

The man that/who I work with never stops talking.

Definite plans: present continuous

Use the present continuous to talk about fixed plans. They often involve other people, and the time/place has been arranged.

When are you starting your new job?
She isn't coming to my birthday party.

➕	I	am	meeting	Alan at 7 P.M.
	He/She/It	is		
	We/You/They	are		
➖	I	am	not meeting	
	He/She/It	is		
	You/We/They	are		
❓	Am	I	meeting	him?
	Is	he/she/it		
	Are	we/you/they		
	Yes, I am./No, I'm not.			

Be going to and the present continuous can be used to express similar ideas. Choose depending on what you mean.

I'm going to see Phil again. (You may or may not have scheduled a definite time and place.)

I'm seeing Phil tonight at the tennis club. (You have scheduled a definite time and place.)

Unit Vocabulary

Cooking and eating

eat out	cook for yourself
diet (noun)	celebrity chef
vegetarian	give (something) up

Adjectives

tasty	delicious	tasteless
awful	disgusting	mouth-watering

Sense verbs

look	feel	sound	smell	taste

UNIT 4
Survival

A

B

C

D

Warm Up

1 **Pair Work** Describe the photos (A–D). What words do you associate with each?

> *A woman is rock climbing. She's high up and holding onto a rock cliff.*
> *With rock climbing, I associate: scary, high, dangerous, exciting, . . .*

2 **Pair Work** Discuss.
1. Which activities in the photos need mental strength, physical strength, or both?
2. What are you afraid of (for example, flying, crowded places, heights, etc.)? Do you do anything to help control your fear? If yes, what?
3. What are your goals at the moment? How will you achieve them?
4. Do you enjoy challenges at work or in your free time? Why or why not?
5. Who do you rely on most in times of need? Why?

Reading

1 Read the articles. Mark the statements below true (*T*), false (*F*), or don't know (*?*).

Going UP

Tenzing Norgay and Sir Edmund Hillary

In 1953, Sir Edmund Hillary and Tenzing Norgay climbed to the top of Mount Everest. The next challenge was to climb it without bottled oxygen. This was the goal of Austrian climbers Peter Habeler and Reinhold Messner. Doctors said they were crazy and told them not to try it. They tried it anyway. On May 8, 1978, they were about 800 meters (2,600 feet) from the top of Everest. They woke at 3 A.M. and began preparing. It took them two hours to get dressed. Every breath was precious,[1] and they used their hands to communicate. Climbing was slow. Messner thought he was going to burst like a balloon. At 8,800 meters (29,000 feet), they stopped and lay down every few steps because of the lack of oxygen. But between one and two in the afternoon they achieved their "impossible" goal. They reached the top of Mount Everest without oxygen.

Most people can hold their breath long enough to dive to the bottom of a swimming pool, but on August 17, 2002, Tanya Streeter went a lot, lot deeper. The 29-year-old held her breath for 3 minutes, 26 seconds and became the world free-diving champion. She dived 160 meters (525 feet) below the surface of the sea. During the dive her lungs shrank[2] to the size of oranges. Her heart slowed to 15 beats a minute, and she sang her national anthem in her head to control her fear. Tanya says that her mental strength is more important than her physical strength. "I am a very determined person. When I decide to do something, I do it. 'Redefine your limits' is my motto."[3]

Going DOWN

Glossary
[1] *precious* = very valuable and important
[2] *to shrink* (past = *shrank*) = to get smaller
[3] *motto* = a phrase that expresses your beliefs

_____ 1. Habeler and Messner didn't listen to doctors.

_____ 2. It took them two hours to go 800 meters.

_____ 3. Tanya Streeter holds the world record for holding her breath.

_____ 4. She was afraid during her dive.

_____ 5. She feels that being physically strong isn't the most important thing.

2 **Group Work** Discuss.

1. Would you like to try free-diving or climbing a mountain like Mount Everest? Why or why not?

2. Do you enjoy watching extreme sports? Are there any extreme sports that you have tried or would like to try?

Vocabulary | describing people

3a Replace the <u>underlined</u> phrases with *be* and an adjective from the box.

> determined   intelligent   confident   ~~brave~~   ambitious   generous   talented   reliable

Ex: My brother <u>isn't afraid of anything</u>. He _is brave._____

1. My aunt <u>gives her money to others</u>. She _____
2. Ako <u>feels sure</u> that she will pass the test. She _____
3. Sarah <u>can understand things quickly</u>. She _____
4. Sandra <u>always does what she says she will do</u>. She _____
5. Joe <u>wants to be successful and powerful</u>. He _____
6. My dad <u>never lets anything stop him</u>. He _____
7. Mei <u>has a lot of natural ability</u> as a writer. She _____

b ▶1.21 Listen and check your answers.

4 **Pair Work** Talk about people you know who have each of the characteristics above.

> *My friend Luis is very generous. He always lends me money.*

Grammar | comparatives

5 Look at these sentences. Then complete the Active Grammar box.

*Habeler and Messner are **stronger than** most people.*
*Free-diving is **more dangerous than** you think.*

Active Grammar

	Adjective	Comparative
One-syllable adjectives	*long* *big*	*longer (than)* *bigger (than)*
Two-syllable adjectives	*boring*	_____
Two-syllable adjectives ending in -*y*	_____	*happier (than)*
Three-syllable adjectives	*determined*	_____
Irregular adjectives	_____ *good*	*worse (than)* _____
Modifiers	*(a little bit/much) taller than*	

See Reference page 46

6 **Pair Work** Find five differences between you and your partner. Then tell other students. Use comparatives.

> *Miyuki is louder than I am.*

Vocabulary | survival skills

1a Match a word or phrase in the box with the <u>underlined</u> words or phrases below.

> **a.** abilities   **b.** deal with   **c.** place to sleep   **d.** try very hard   **e.** nature

_____ 1. How long do you think you could survive in <u>the wilderness</u>?

_____ 2. What survival <u>skills</u> do you have?

_____ 3. Could you build a <u>shelter</u> in a forest?

_____ 4. Do you usually <u>push yourself</u> in difficult situations?

_____ 5. Do you <u>cope with</u> new situations well (for example, moving to a different city)?

b **Pair Work** Ask and answer the questions above.

Listening

2a **Pair Work** Look at the ad below. What do you think students will do at this school?

b ▶1.22 Listen to a talk by David Johnson, the head instructor at the Hillside Survival School. Check your answer to Exercise 2a.

3 Listen again and complete the notes below.

4 **Pair Work** Discuss. Would you like to take one of the courses at the Hillside Survival School? Why or why not?

Hillside
SURVIVAL SCHOOL
Learn to cope in the wilderness!

THE HILLSIDE SURVIVAL SCHOOL

1. David's previous work: _____
2. His "aims": help people discover nature/outdoor life; _____

Basic survival course:
3. How long? _____
4. When does it take place? _____
5. Cost? _____

Extreme survival course:
6. When does it take place? _____
7. Cost? _____

8. Minimum age: _____
9. Full payment by: _____
10. Discounts for: _____

Grammar | superlatives

5 Read this note about the course. Do the writers feel positive or negative?

Hi David,

Just a quick email to say we really enjoyed the weekend. It was one of the <u>hardest</u> things we've ever done but also one of the <u>most exciting</u>. Thanks a million for an experience we will never forget (even though you said our shelter was the <u>worst</u> you've ever seen)!

Best wishes,

Catherine and Wen

6 Look at the <u>underlined</u> words in Exercise 5. How do you form superlatives? Complete the Active Grammar box.

Active Grammar

1. **Short adjectives (one syllable):**
   the + adjective + _____

2. **Long adjectives (two or more syllables):**
   the + _____ + adjective

3. **Two-syllable adjectives ending in -*y*:**
   the + adjective (without -*y*) + -*iest*

4. **Irregular adjectives:**
   good = *best*   *bad* = _____

5. Before superlatives we use *the* or a possessive.
   the oldest building   *my best friend*

See Reference page 46

7 Write sentences using the superlative form of the adjectives.

Ex: This/comfortable chair/in the house.   <u>*This is the most comfortable chair in the house.*</u>

1. Everest/high/mountain/in the world. _____
2. What/good department store/in New York? _____
3. This/wet day/of the year so far. _____
4. This/boring movie/I have ever seen. _____
5. Soccer/popular sport/in Brazil. _____

Pronunciation | sentence stress

8a <u>Underline</u> the words in each sentence in Exercise 7 that would usually be stressed.

This is the most <u>comfortable</u> <u>chair</u> in the <u>house</u>.

b ▶1.23 Listen and check your answers.

Speaking

9 **Pair Work** Discuss.

1. What is the most dangerous situation you've ever been in? What happened?
2. What is the most interesting place you've been to?
3. Who is your best friend? Why is he or she your best friend?

Writing

10 Look at the thank you note in Exercise 5. Think of a real reason for a thank you note. Write the thank you note.

Reading

1a **Pair Work** What words come to mind when you think about England and the English?

b Read the article. Circle the topics in the box that are mentioned.

> being polite   soccer   drinking tea
> English food   libraries   driving habits
> the weather

Looking at . . . England

There are ideas about England and the English that are just not true. England does not stop for afternoon tea every day, although the English do drink a lot of the liquid (hot, with milk), and although the weather is very changeable, it doesn't rain all the time!

Also, there's a lot of good food in England. No, really! In the major cities you'll find the cuisine of almost every nationality. Indian food is a particular favorite of the English. To find classic English food, try eating in a traditional pub.

The famous English politeness is everywhere. The English use "Please," "Thank you," and "Sorry" more than most nationalities. For example, if you step on someone's foot, they'll probably say "Sorry" to you! If you make a complaint, it's also common to begin with "Sorry" as in: "I'm sorry, but this soup is cold."

You may think it strange on the London Underground that people don't talk to each other, even when crowded together in the rush hour. Silence is normal, as people read their books or newspapers. That doesn't mean English people are unfriendly. It just means you might have to get to know them first!

British English	American English
underground	subway

2 Mark the statements true (*T*) or false (*F*). Correct the false statements.

_____ 1. The English don't like their tea to be hot.

_____ 2. You get a lot of different types of weather in England.

_____ 3. Indian food is very popular in England.

_____ 4. You can find typical English food in top restaurants.

_____ 5. The English often use "Sorry" to begin a complaint.

_____ 6. The English like to talk to strangers on the Underground.

3 **Pair Work** Discuss. What do you think a short article about your country might mention?

Listening

4a ▶1.24 Listen to three conversations and answer the questions.

Conversation 1: Where does she want to go? _____

What does she want the driver to do? _____

Conversation 2: What does the customer ask for? _____

What does the salesperson do? _____

Conversation 3: Where does the passenger want to go? _____

Does the driver know where it is? _____

b **Pair Work** Look at the Audioscripts on page 141. Practice the conversations with another student.

Grammar | indirect questions

5 Look at the Active Grammar box. Complete rules 1 and 2. Then answer the following questions:

1. What happens to the verbs in indirect questions?
2. How do you make direct *Yes/No* questions indirect?

Active Grammar

Use indirect questions when you want to be polite.

Direct question	Indirect question
How far **is** the station?	**Do you know** how far the station **is**?
Where **can** I **get** a taxi?	**Could you tell me** where I **can get** a taxi?
What time **does** the train **arrive**?	**Do you know** what time the train **arrives**?
Is the museum open?	**Do you know if** the museum **is** open?

1. Indirect questions with *be*:
   question word + *subject*
   + _____

2. Indirect questions with main verbs:
   question word +
   _____ + _____

See Reference page 46

6 Make these questions indirect. Use the words in parentheses.

Ex: How long does the trip take? (Do you know?)   _Do you know how long the trip takes?_

1. How much is that? (Could you tell me?) _____
2. Where can I get an application form? (Do you know?) _____
3. Do you have any postage stamps? (Do you know?) _____
4. How far is it to the library? (Do you know?) _____
5. Is there a post office near here? (Could you tell me?) _____
6. What time is it? (Do you know?) _____

Speaking

7a You're going to interview a classmate for a market research company. Choose a topic from the box.

free-time activities	vacations
Internet use	shopping
favorite movies	food

b **Pair Work** Look at the How To box. Then conduct your interview. When you're finished, report your findings to the class.

How To:	
Be polite in English	
Use polite words/phrases	• *Excuse me, could I ask you a few questions?* • *Could you say that again, please?*
Use indirect questions	• *Could you tell me what kinds of movies you like?*

Review

1 Complete these sentences with comparatives. Use the adjectives in the box.

> quiet   bad   exciting   ~~old~~   close   happy

Ex: She is only 23. I thought she was __older__.

1. This restaurant is very noisy. Can we go somewhere _____?
2. That movie sounds really boring. *Murder City* sounds _____.
3. My job is pretty good. It could be a lot _____.
4. You seem _____ today—you looked sad yesterday.
5. The house was _____ to the station than I thought.

2 Complete these sentences with superlatives. Use the adjectives in the box.

> tall   friendly   expensive   fast   ~~long~~   hot

Ex: It's __the longest__ movie I've ever seen. It lasted four hours!

1. This jacket cost $850. It was _____ one in the shop!
2. August is usually _____ month in China.
3. Eduardo is _____ boy in the class. He is almost six feet tall.
4. This is _____ car I've ever had. It drives like a race car.
5. Michael is _____ man I've ever met. He loves to meet new people.

3 Add a word to each sentence to make it correct.

Ex: Can you tell me where the bathroom $\overset{is}{\wedge}$?

1. You know why he isn't home yet?
2. Do you know I can pay by credit card?
3. Could you tell me I can find a gas station?
4. Could you tell whose car this is, please?
5. Do you know time the next train leaves?

4 Ask about the following things using *Do you know . . . ?* or *Could you tell me . . . ?* Then practice asking and answering with a partner.

Ex: what time/mall close?   *Do you know what time the mall closes?*

1. where/find/cheap hotel?   _____
2. nice restaurant/near here?   _____
3. how much/taxi to the airport?   _____
4. where/I/buy/map of Bangkok?   _____
5. need visa/go to Ireland?   _____

Communication | agree on choices with a partner

5 Which of these things can you see in the photos?

rope	shovel	blankets	chocolate	box of matches
axe	water	flashlight	pocket knife	pen and paper
tent	mirror	umbrella	first-aid kit	
radio	candles	scissors	plastic bowl	

6 ▶1.25 Listen and answer the questions.
  1. Where are they talking about surviving?
     a. in a forest   b. in a desert
  2. List the items they decide to take.
     _____ _____ _____
     _____ _____

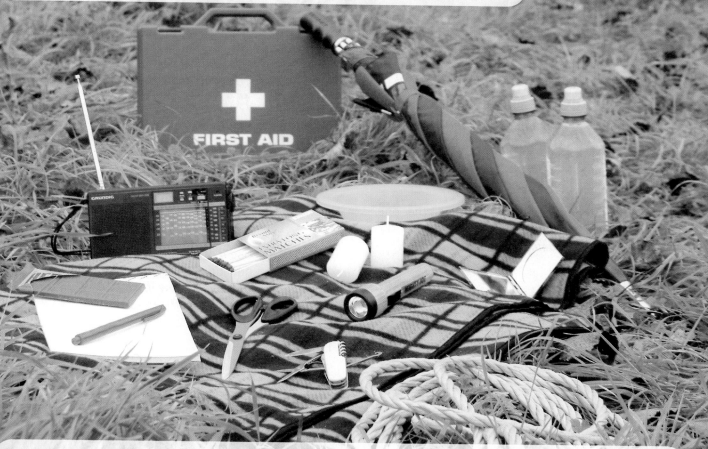

7 Read the Audioscript on page 141. What language do they use to:
  1. express their opinions? _____
  2. make suggestions? _____
  3. make comparisons? _____

8 **Group Work** Choose one of the places from Exercise 6. Then discuss which five objects from Exercise 5 you will take to help you survive.

Unit 4 Reference

Comparatives and superlatives

One-syllable adjectives

Adjective	Comparative	Superlative	Spelling
hard	harder (than)	the hardest	ends in consonant: + -er; the -est
nice brave	nicer (than) braver (than)	the nicest the bravest	ends in -e: + -r; the -est
sad big	sadder bigger	the saddest the biggest	vowel + consonant: double consonant

Their yard is **larger than** ours.
Brian is **the thinnest** boy in the class.

Two- or more syllable adjectives

Adjective	Comparative	Superlative	Spelling
happy easy	happier (than) easier (than)	the happiest the easiest	two syllables, ends in -y: y changes to i
boring interesting	**more** boring (than) **more** interesting (than)	**the most** boring **the most** interesting	two or more syllables: no change

This beach is **more crowded than** the other one.
It's **the easiest** way to do it.
She is **the most famous** person I know.

Irregular adjectives

Adjective	Comparative	Superlative
bad	worse (than)	(the) worst
good	better (than)	(the) best

(not) as . . . as
Make comparisons with *(not) as . . . as.*

> Marta is **as tall as** Tom, but she **isn't as tall as** Rachel.

Before superlatives
Use *the* or a possessive adjective.

> **the** least expensive   **my** oldest son

After superlatives
We usually use *in* with places and groups of people:

> What is the highest mountain **in** the world?

Use *of* in most other cases:

> She is the smartest **of** my three sisters.

We often use the present perfect:

> He's the most interesting person I'**ve** ever **met**.

Indirect questions

Use indirect questions to make a question more polite.

> Who are those people? →
> **Could you tell me** who those people are?
> When will you arrive? →
> **Do you know** when you will arrive?

Use the word order of positive statements.

> Could you tell me what time **the store opens**?

Drop the auxiliaries *do/does/did.*

> How much **do the tickets cost**? →
> Do you know how much **the tickets cost**?

Use *if* or *whether* for indirect *Yes/No* questions.

> Do you know **if/whether** Mr. Barnard is in his office?

Unit Vocabulary

Survival
achieve your goal   survive in the wilderness
control your fear   cope with new situations
push yourself   physical/mental strength
skills   shelter   rely on

Survival equipment

axe	shovel	blankets
tent	mirror	first-aid kit
rope	scissors	box of matches
candles	flashlight	pocket knife

Describing people
ambitious   brave   confident   determined
generous   reliable   talented   intelligent

UNIT 5
Life events

A

B

C

D

Warm Up

1   Look at the photos. What are the people doing? How old are they?

2   What is the typical age in your country to do the things below?

get married	have children	earn a good salary	look after your grandchildren
retire	get engaged	graduate from college	get a place of your own
get a job	leave home	learn to drive a car	

3   **Pair Work** Briefly describe your life or the life of an older person.

> *My grandmother was born in Monterrey in 1952. When she was a child, she moved to Mexico City. She got married in her 20s . . .*

Reading

1 **Pair Work** Discuss.

1. Describe the situations in the photos. Have you ever had similar experiences?
2. What has (have) been the best year(s) of your life so far? Why?

2a Read the profile.

FROM ADOLESCENT TO ADULT

Fei is an only child and lives with her family in Shanghai. She is studying law at Jiaotong University, and she will turn 18 in a few weeks.

My goals are to get my degree, to go to Australia to study marketing, and then to come back and find a good job. China is changing, and you can earn a lot of money now in China.

When I'm earning a good salary, I'd like to do more traveling, but I have to take care of my parents, too. They're going to retire soon. They've given me a good life, and I have to do the same for them. This is the way things are in China, and it should be the same everywhere.

Usually, when you get married, you're only allowed to have one child. However, because I'm an only child, I can have two children if I marry another only child. Anyway, at the moment it's all a dream, because I'm single.

I like reading stories on the Internet. I also like reading fashion magazines like *Vogue*. I think my favorite thing is to go shopping with my friends. We can't afford to buy much, but it's fun to look in the windows and think about what we're going to buy when we have more money!

b **Pair Work** Take turns asking and answering the questions with a partner.

1. What does Fei hope to do in the future?
2. Why does she want to find a job in China after finishing school?
3. Why does she feel she should take care of her parents?
4. How many children can most couples in China have?
5. Why might Fei be able to have two children?
6. Why do Fei and her friends like to go window-shopping?

Grammar | modals of obligation: *should, can, have to*

3 Read the examples in the Active Grammar box and complete the explanations with the underlined modals.

> ### Active Grammar
>
> I **have to** take care of them.
> I **don't have to** work abroad.
>
> You **can** earn a lot of money.
> We **can't** afford to buy much.
>
> It **should** be less expensive.
> She **shouldn't** spend so much.
>
> 1. Use _____ to say something is possible.
> 2. Use _____ to say something is necessary.
> 3. Use _____ to say something is a good idea.
> 4. Use _____ to say something isn't possible.
> 5. Use _____ to say something isn't necessary.
> 6. Use _____ to say something isn't a good idea.

See Reference page 56

4 Complete these sentences with *should(n't), can('t),* or *(don't) have to*.

Ex: I __*have to*__ get good grades so I can go to college.

1. You _____ spend the night at my place. We have a spare bedroom.
2. Young people in my country _____ do military service. It stopped last year.
3. I think everyone _____ vote in elections. It's our duty as citizens.
4. I think people _____ come to work in jeans. It looks bad.

Pronunciation | contractions *shouldn't* and *can't*

5 ▶1.26 Listen to these sentences. Is the final *t* of *shouldn't* and *can't* pronounced?

1. She <u>shouldn't</u> ask that.
2. I <u>can't</u> buy that.

6 **Pair Work** Take turns making sentences about your country. Use *should(n't), can('t),* or *(don't) have to*. Include your opinion.

Ex: people/vote

> In the US, people can't vote until they're 18 years old, but they don't have to vote. I think everyone should vote.

Listening and Speaking

7 ▶1.27 Listen to two conversations. Which two statements are they discussing?

1. Eighteen is too young to get married.
2. Teenagers only think about dating and money.
3. Young people should do military service.

8 Listen again. Circle any phrases in the How To box that you hear.

9 **Group Work** Give your opinions on the three statements in Exercise 7.

How To:

Exchange opinions with a friend	
1. Give your opinion	I think / I don't think . . . In my opinion . . .
2. Explain why	because . . . I mean . . .
3. Ask for an opinion	What do you think? Don't you think so?
4. Agree/disagree	You're probably right . . . I don't know. I'm not so sure . . .

Write a personal profile

GRAMMAR present perfect with *for* and *since*

Grammar | present perfect with *for* and *since*

1 Read the website profile. Then look at the <u>underlined</u> words and answer the questions below.

Friends Together

American English	British English
apartment downtown	flat the centre of town

Ana Silva

What I'm doing now

Since I graduated from college, I've traveled a little bit and had a few different jobs, including working on a cruise ship in the Caribbean. But <u>I've worked for the same company for the last two years</u> now, and I really like it. It's a big advertising firm, and I'm an Accounts Manager.

<u>I've lived in São Paulo since 2010</u> and have a small apartment downtown that I share with Gerald, my cat!

I haven't seen anyone from school for ages, so send me a message. I'd love to hear from you!

Send an email to Ana
Send an ecard to Ana
Send a voice message to Ana

1. When did Ana start her job? _____

2. Does she still work there? _____

3. When did Ana move to São Paulo?

_____

2 Complete the Active Grammar box with the past participle of the verbs in parentheses. Then complete the rules below with *for* or *since*.

1. Use _____ to refer to the start of the action.

2. Use _____ to refer to the time period of the action.

3a Read the conversation between Ana and an old friend, Martin. Complete, using *for* or *since*.

Ana: I'm so glad you emailed. It's been ages _____ (1.) I've heard from you!

Martin: I know. Well, I've been in Tokyo _____ (2.) almost two years. I'm teaching English here.

Ana: So, are you enjoying it?

Martin: Yes, it's great. Especially _____ (3.) I met this woman named Emmy. We've known each other _____ (4.) about six months now. She works in the same school as me.

Ana: Oh! That's great . . . So, when are you both coming to São Paulo?

b ▶1.28 Listen and check your answers.

Active Grammar

Remember: Form the present perfect with *have/has* + past participle

➕ 1. My dad has _____ (be) in the hospital **for** a week.

➖ 2. We haven't _____ (see) her **since** college.

❓ 3. Have you _____ (live) in Paris **for** long?

See Reference page 56 and irregular verb list on page 138

Speaking

4 **Pair Work** Think of three people or things that are important to you. Talk about how long you have known the people or have had the things.

> *I have known my best friend, Sam, for 15 years.*

Vocabulary | friendship

5 Match the words or phrases with the correct definitions.

_____ 1. a colleague   a. have a good relationship

_____ 2. an old friend   b. someone you work with

_____ 3. get in touch   c. have no more contact

_____ 4. go out (with someone)   d. start having contact

_____ 5. get along well (with someone)   e. someone you met a long time ago

_____ 6. lose touch   f. go on a date with someone

6 Complete Ana's message with the correct form of the words or phrases from Exercise 5.

Martin is _____ (1.) of mine. I met him in high school. We _____ (2.). In fact, we were best friends. But after school we _____ (3.), and I didn't hear from him for years. About a year ago, I got on Friends Together. Martin saw my profile and _____ (4.) again. He used to _____ (5.) with a woman named Emmy. She was his _____ (6.)—they worked at the same school. But they broke up, and Martin is coming to visit me in Brazil next week.

7 **Pair Work** Look at the pictures. Decide on a possible order and think of a story using the phrases from Exercise 5. Then take turns telling your stories.

> *Mateo was Karen's boyfriend in high school. She . . .*

Writing

8 Write your own profile. Use Ana's profile as a model.

Speaking

1a **Pair Work** Ask and answer the questions to complete the quiz.

LIVING LONGER
HOW MUCH DO YOU KNOW?

1 On average, which nationality lives the longest?
  a. the Japanese
  b. the Canadians
  c. the Swedish

2 What was the average lifespan 2,000 years ago?
  a. 26 years
  b. 36 years
  c. 46 years

3 By 2050, what percentage of the world's population will be 65 or older?
  a. 2% b. 10% c. 20%

4 On average, which groups of people live longer?
  a. smokers or non-smokers?
  b. single people or married people?
  c. pet owners or non-pet owners?

b ▶1.29 Listen and check the answers. Do any of them surprise you?

2 **Pair Work** Discuss. Which statement do you agree with more?
  1. How long you live depends on your lifestyle (diet, exercise, smoking, etc.).
  2. How long you live depends on your genes.

Grammar | past routines: *used to*

3 Match the person to the reason they give for living a long time.

> getting exercise   mental activity   thinking positively

"I'm 89 years old. I used to play a lot of sports, but I don't play any now. The most important thing for me is to feel good about life and laugh every day." _____

"I'll be 80 on my next birthday. The thing that keeps me young is dancing. I didn't use to get any exercise, but now I dance every day." _____

"I can't believe it, but I'm 87! I used to smoke, but I gave it up when I was 55. I don't get much exercise, but I like to keep my brain active. I love chess." _____

4 Look at the quotes in Exercise 3 and complete the Active Grammar box with *use* or *used*.

5 Complete the sentences with *used to* or *didn't use to*.

1. (have) I _____ long hair, but now it's short.
2. (be) We _____ friends, but now we're not.
3. (work) Paul _____ for me, but now he's my boss.
4. (not be) Sophia _____ into fashion, but now she is.
5. (you/play) _____ any sports in school?
6. (not like) I _____ olives, but now I do.
7. (they/live) _____ together?

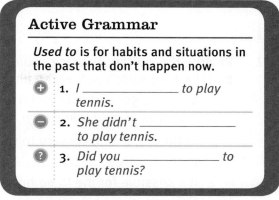

Active Grammar

Used to is for habits and situations in the past that don't happen now.

➕ 1. I _____ to play tennis.

➖ 2. She didn't _____ to play tennis.

❓ 3. Did you _____ to play tennis?

See Reference page 56

Pronunciation | *used to/didn't use to*

6 ▶1.30 Listen to the first two sentences from Exercise 5. How do you pronounce *used to* and *didn't use to*? Practice saying sentences 1–7 with the correct pronunciation.

Vocabulary | habits

7a Match a verb from A with a noun phrase from B.

A	B
____ 1. eat	a. a heavy smoker
____ 2. eat	b. mentally active
____ 3. be	c. a lot of exercise
____ 4. be	d. junk food
____ 5. drink	e. to bed very late
____ 6. go	f. a lot of water
____ 7. think	g. healthy food
____ 8. get	h. positively

b **Pair Work** Discuss.

1. Which of the verb phrases do you think are good habits? Which are bad?
2. Which of the things did you use to do? Which do you do now?

Speaking

8 **Pair Work** Tell your partner about when you were younger. Think about the topics in the box.

I used to want to be a pilot, but now I'm afraid of flying!

sports	likes and dislikes
pets	hair and clothes
music	hopes and fears

Review

1 Rewrite the sentences using *should(n't), can('t),* or *(don't) have to*. With a partner, take turns reading the answers.

> **Ex:** It's a good idea to join a gym if you want to get in shape.
> <u>*You should join a gym if you want to get in shape.*</u>

1. In the US, it is necessary to wear seatbelts.
   In the US, you _____.

2. It's possible for me to do my homework while I watch TV.
   I _____.

3. It's a good idea to get a good guidebook before you leave for Europe.
   You _____.

4. It's not necessary to drive me to the airport.
   You _____.

5. It's not a good idea to drink coffee just before you go to bed.
   You _____.

6. It's not possible for me to finish this report today.
   I _____.

2 Complete the following sentences with *for* or *since*.

> **Ex:** I've known Susie <u>*since*</u> we were in elementary school.

1. She's lived in Lima _____ years!

2. We haven't had this car _____ very long.

3. They've worked there _____ 2005.

4. I've had this watch _____ last summer.

3 Rewrite each item as one sentence, using the present perfect and *for* or *since*.

> **Ex:** Sam works for our company. He joined six months ago.
> <u>*Sam has worked for our company for six months.*</u>

1. I play the guitar. I began when I was a child. _____

2. My parents live in Boston. They moved there in April. _____

3. I have a dog. I got him two years ago. _____

4. Ten years ago they went on vacation.
   They didn't go on vacation after that. _____

5. I study English. I started three years ago. _____

4 Find the mistakes and rewrite the sentences correctly.

> **Ex:** I didn't use like my piano teacher. <u>*I didn't use to like my piano teacher.*</u>

1. Did you use play football in school? _____

2. She didn't to get good grades. _____

3. Where you use to live? _____

4. I used like my job more than I do now. _____

5. My parents didn't use have a computer. _____

Communication | make a simple informal presentation

5 **Pair Work** Discuss. What do you know about Johnny Depp?

6a ▶ 1.31 Listen to a show called *Biography Break*. What is the importance of the information below?

Kentucky	20 times	age 12	*21 Jump Street*	age 16
hobbies	houses	age 20	Nicholas Cage	

b **Pair Work** Use the information in the box to take turns telling about Johnny Depp's life.

> *Johnny Depp was born in Kentucky.*

7 **Pair Work** You're going to make a short presentation about your partner. Ask your partner questions about the topics below. Take notes for your presentation.

place of birth	childhood	education	successes in life
relationships	career	hobbies	language-learning history

> *What was your childhood like?*

8 **Group Work** Make your presentation to your group or class.

> *James was born in Honolulu. His family moved to . . .*

Unit 5 Reference

should, can, have to

should, can

Form: modal verb + base form		
(+) I/You He/She/It We/They	should can	wait.
(−) I/You He/She/It We/They	shouldn't can't	smoke.
(?) Should/ Shouldn't Can/Can't	I/you/he/ she/it/we/they	go?

Use *should(n't)* when you think something is a good/bad idea.

> You **should arrive** early for a job interview.
> You **shouldn't stay** up late before an important exam.

Use *can('t)* when something is possible/impossible.

> I **can't unlock** the door with this key.

have to

Form: modal verb + base form		
(+) I/You/We/They	have to	work.
He/She/It	has to	
(−) I/You/We/They	don't have to	come.
He/She/It	doesn't have to	
(?) Do	I/you/we/they have to	leave?
Does	he/she/it have to	

Use *have to* when something is necessary and there is no choice.

> I **have to get** up early tomorrow, because my train leaves at 7.

Use *don't have to* when something is not necessary and there is a choice.

> You **don't have to go** to the party.

Present perfect with *for* and *since*

Use the present perfect with *for* and *since* to talk about actions or states of being that started in the past and continue to now.

> I**'ve lived** in this country for six years.
> I **haven't seen** Maria since last summer.

Use *for* to give the length of the time.

> for three years, for a week, for half an hour

Use *since* to give the beginning of the time.

> since 1996, since this morning, since 10:30

used to

Form: *used to* + base form			
(+) I/You He/She We/They	used to	play the piano.	
(−) I/You He/She We/They	didn't use to	do any exercise.	
(?) Did	I/you he/she we/they	use to	live there?

Used to refers to regular activities and states of being in the past that don't happen now.

> Tina **used to play** the violin, but now she doesn't.
> I **didn't use to like** goat cheese, but now I love it.

Unit Vocabulary

Life activities

retire	have children
get a job	get engaged/married
graduate	get a place of your own
learn to drive	earn a good salary

Friendship

lose touch	get in touch
old friend	get along well (with someone)
colleague	go out (with someone)

Good and bad habits

get exercise	be a heavy smoker
eat junk food	be mentally active
think positively	go to bed very late
eat healthy food	

UNIT 6
Destinations

A

B

C

D

Warm Up

1a **Pair Work** Look at the photos and the country names below. Which country do you think each picture shows? Discuss.

Spain	Italy	Brazil	France	Japan	Canada	Colombia	Germany
Korea	Peru	China	Kenya	Britain	Mexico	Australia	the United States

b Which countries have you visited? Which would you like to visit most? Why?

2a Write the nationality for each country from the box in Exercise 1.

Spain—Spanish

b ▶1.32 Underline the stressed syllable in each word. Then listen and check.

Listening

1a **Pair Work** Complete the map (1–7) with the words in the box. Which words **can't** you use?

> Lake   Beach   Island   Desert   River
> Sea   Ocean   Forest   Mountain

b ▶1.33 Listen and check your answers.

2a **Pair Work** Decide on the correct information about New Zealand.

1. The population is *4 million/40 million*.
2. The number of sheep is *4 million/40 million*.
3. The capital of New Zealand is *Auckland/Wellington*.
4. The national symbol is a *kiwi bird/kiwi fruit*.
5. You can do water sports on the *North Island/South Island*.
6. You can go skiing on the *North Island/ South Island*.

b ▶1.34 Listen to the tour guide and check your answers.

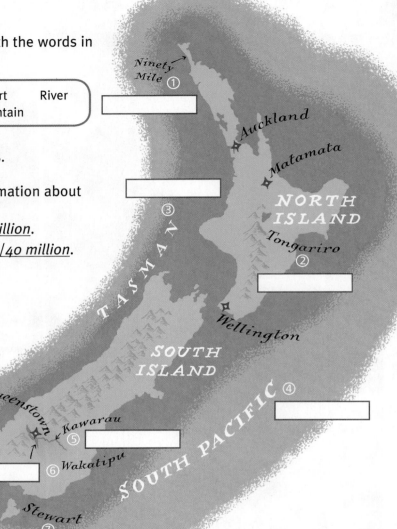

Reading

3 **Pair Work** Read the article on the next page. Then ask and answer the questions below.

1. What is the LOTR effect?
2. Why do tourists visit Matamata?
3. By what percent do experts think tourism will increase in the near future?
4. How might increased tourism hurt New Zealand?

4 **Pair Work** Find these underlined words and phrases in the article and say what they refer to.

Ex: they (line 6)   *the islands of New Zealand*

1. it (line 13)   3. they (line 20)   5. these things (line 32)
2. that (line 17)   4. it (line 25)

For years, many people thought that New Zealand was famous for sheep, rugby, and . . . more sheep. But
5 suddenly these islands have a new image. <u>They</u> are now one of the most fashionable tourist destinations in the world. And it's all because
10 of a movie, or actually three movies. *The Lord of the Rings* series was filmed in New Zealand, and <u>it</u>'s a wonderful ad for the country. People now
15 want to visit New Zealand to see the places in the movies. Tourism in New Zealand is doing very well—<u>that</u>'s the LOTR effect. Some tourists come just to see the movie locations. For example, there's a beautiful place called Matamata just south of Auckland, and 250 tourists come
20 here every day. <u>They</u> pay 30 dollars each to see the remains of Hobbiton village from the first *The Lord of the Rings* movie.

In the two weeks after the first movie came out, travel to New Zealand increased by more than 20 percent. Experts think that the number of tourists will double in the near future, and

25 <u>it</u> won't stop there. Some people think that New Zealand will soon have over 3 million tourists a year. But there are some questions about all this success. Will tourism change the natural beauty of the landscape? Will it affect the
30 wildlife? And will tourists still want to visit New Zealand if <u>these things</u> happen?

Mount Ngauruhoe was "Mount Doom" in LOTR.

American English	British English
movie	film
ad	advert

Grammar | *will*

5 Look at the Active Grammar box and complete the examples.

6 Complete the sentences with *will* (*'ll*) or *won't* and a verb from the box.

be	pass	rain
go	see	hurt

1. I don't want to go to that beach. It _____ crowded today.
2. We don't have much money, so we _____ on vacation this year.
3. I _____ the whole country in two weeks. It's too big.
4. Don't worry about your driving test. I'm sure you _____ .
5. The weather doesn't look very good. Do you think it _____ ?
6. Don't be scared of my dog. He _____ you.

Active Grammar

Use *will* (+ verb) to make predictions about the future.

The negative of *will* is *won't* (*will not*).

(+) 1. *The number of tourists _____ _____ (double) in the near future.*

(−) 2. *It _____ _____ (not stop) there.*

(?) 3. *_____ tourism _____ (change) the natural beauty of the landscape?*

See Reference page 66

Speaking

7 **SPEAKING EXCHANGE** Go to page 131 and answer the questions with a partner.

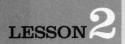
Listening

1a Look at the photo and read the TV guide excerpt. What is the show *Frontier House* about?

An American frontier family in the 1800s

Frontier House

Channel 4 • 7:30 P.M.

Can modern people cope with 19th-century life? The Clune family from California decided to find out. For six months the parents and their four children lived like Americans in the Wild West over 100 years ago.

What did they find difficult? How did the experience change them? Watch *Frontier House* and find out how modern people cope with old-fashioned life.

b **Pair Work** Try to predict what each family member will find difficult about being in *Frontier House*.

Father	
Mother	
Teenage girls	
Boys (ages nine and eleven)	

2a ▶1·35 Listen to two people talking about *Frontier House* and check if your predictions in Exercise 1b were correct.

b Listen again and circle the correct choice.
1. They lived in the style of people in about *1818/1880*.
2. The nearest store was *six/sixteen* kilometers away.
3. The father became *thinner/ill*.
4. The mother *missed/didn't miss* her make-up.
5. At first, the children *liked/didn't like* having so much to do.
6. The girls missed *shopping/TV* the most.
7. At the end of the experience, Tracy said her clothes were *more/less* important to her.

3 ▶1·36 What do you think happened when they went home? Listen and see if you were right.

4 **Group Work** Discuss.
1. Would you like to be in a TV show like *Frontier House*? Why or why not?
2. Which country would you like to live in for six months, (a) now? (b) 100 years ago? Give your reasons.

Grammar | adverbs: *too, too much/many, enough*

5a Look at the two sentences. Is the meaning the same or different?

He was *too weak*. He *wasn't strong enough*.

b Match the rules and the examples in the Active Grammar box.

Active Grammar

_____ 1. Use *too* with adjectives and adverbs.

_____ 2. Use *too much* with non-count nouns.

_____ 3. Use *too many* with count nouns.

_____ 4. Use (*not*) *enough* after adjectives and adverbs.

_____ 5. Use (*not*) *enough* before nouns.

a. *They weren't warm enough.*

b. *I'm too tired to do any more work today.*

c. *I had too much time and nothing to do.*

d. *They often didn't have enough food.*

e. *There were too many things to do.*

See Reference page 66

6 Complete these sentences using the words in parentheses and *enough, too, too much,* or *too many.*

Ex: My coat isn't ___*warm enough*___ for me. (warm)

1. I'm very tired. I went to bed _____ last night. (late)

2. I'm very busy today. I have _____ to do. (things)

3. I didn't have _____ to do my homework yesterday. (time)

4. I often spend _____ on clothes. (money)

Vocabulary | machines at home

7 Label the pictures. Use words and phrases from the box.

American English	British English
stove	cooker

MP3 player   dishwasher   stove
hairdryer   vacuum cleaner

Speaking

8 ▶1.37 Listen. What is the task? What do the people agree on?

9 **Pair Work** Have a discussion like the one in Exercise 8. Use the How To box to help you.

How To:

Talk about choices	
1. State your choice	*I'd like to choose . . .* *I think we should take . . .*
2. Give a general reason . . .	*because . . .* *The main reason is that . . .*
3. Add a personal reason	*I couldn't live without it!* *I'm too lazy to . . .*

Reading

1 **Pair Work** What do you know about Nelson Mandela? Discuss.

> *He was in prison for a long time.*

2 Match the pictures (A–D) on the brochure with the phrases. Then read the brochure.

> _____ water plants   _____ plant seeds   _____ harvest the fruit/vegetables   _____ get rid of weeds

Garden of Freedom

The charity *Seeds for Africa* has started its first prison vegetable garden at Kabwe Prison in Zambia. There are 500 prisoners at Kabwe Prison, and the prison garden will give them fresh vegetables to eat. More importantly, the prison staff hope that the garden will increase the prisoners' self-esteem.[1] The Kabwe Prison garden was inspired by Nelson Mandela, who spent 27 years in prison in South Africa. Gardening helped Mandela to increase his self-esteem.

"My garden was my way of escaping what surrounded us. I looked at all the empty space we had on the roof and how it got sun the whole day.

"I decided I'd like to start a garden, and after years of asking, I received permission.[2] I asked for 16 large oil drums and asked the staff to cut them in half for me. They then filled each half with soil and created 32 giant flowerpots.

"A garden was one of the few things in prison that I could control. It gave me the simple but important satisfaction of planting a seed, watching it grow, watering it, and then harvesting it. It was a small taste of freedom. In some ways, I saw the garden as being like my life. A leader must also look after his garden; he, too, plants seeds and then watches, cultivates,[3] and harvests the result."

(adapted from *Long Walk to Freedom* by Nelson Mandela)

To find out more about the prison garden and other projects, go to **www.seedsforafrica.org**

> **Glossary**
> [1] *self-esteem* = feeling good about yourself
> [2] *receive permission* = someone in authority says you can do something
> [3] *cultivate* = prepare and use land for growing plants

3 **Pair Work** Take turns asking and answering the questions.

1. Who started the garden in Kabwe prison?
2. How did gardening help Mandela?
3. What is the main reason for the garden at Kabwe prison?
4. Why did Mandela start his garden?
5. Why was the garden a "small taste of freedom"?
6. What does Mandela compare the garden to?

Grammar | uses of *like*

4a Match the questions and the answers in the Active Grammar box.

> ### Active Grammar
>
> _____ 1. What **do you like to** do in your free time?
> _____ 2. What **would you like to** do today?
> _____ 3. What **is** your garden **like**?
> _____ 4. What **does** your garden **look like**?
>
> a. I'd like to start a garden.
> b. I like gardening.
> c. It's very colorful.
> d. It's very peaceful.

See Reference page 66

b Match the definitions with the different uses of *like*.

_____ 1. want or want to do   a. be like
_____ 2. enjoy   b. like
_____ 3. appearance   c. look like
_____ 4. character or characteristics d. would like

Pronunciation | reductions

5 ▶1.38 Listen to sentences 1–2 in the Active Grammar box. How are *What do you* and *would you* pronounced?

6 **Pair Work** Write questions using *like*, *look like*, *would like to*, or *be like*. Then ask and answer the questions.

Ex: Do you enjoy gardening?   *Do you like gardening?*

1. Tell me about your best friend. _____
2. Do you want to go out tonight? _____
3. Tell me about your best friend's appearance. _____

Writing

7 **Pair Work** What is your favorite natural place (for example, a garden, a beach, a forest)? What's it like? Make notes about this place. Then tell your partner about it.

8 Read the description in the Writing bank on page 135. Do the exercises, and then write about your favorite place.

Review

1 Complete the sentences using *'ll/won't* and a verb from the box.

~~close~~   not/forget   have   help   pay   stay   not/walk

Ex: It's cold in here. I think I'_ll close_____ the window.

1. **A:** What would you like?
   B: I _____ a cheese sandwich, please.

2. **A:** I promise I _____ to buy some milk.
   B: Great. Thanks!

3. **A:** I _____ to work today—it's too wet.
   B: Do you want to share a taxi?

4. **A:** Do you want to go out tonight?
   B: No, I think I _____ in.

5. **A:** Thanks for the money. I _____ you back tomorrow.
   B: OK. No problem. Glad to help.

6. **A:** This homework is too difficult.
   B: I _____ you.

2 Put the words in the correct order.

Ex: don't go on money to have enough vacation I
   I don't have enough money to go on vacation.

1. food to The eat too was hot   _____

2. coffee isn't enough There my sugar in   _____

3. far to walk too home here It's from   _____

4. get She's old married not enough to   _____

5. pool the There many in too people were   _____

6. too chocolate eat Don't much   _____

3 Look at the answers and write questions with *like*, using the cues. Then ask a partner the questions. Give your own answers.

Ex: (you/on weekends)
   A: _What do you like doing on weekends?_
   B: I like going shopping with my friends.

1. (you/for your next vacation)
   A: _____?
   B: I'd like to go to Ecuador.

2. (your street)
   A: _____?
   B: It's quiet, but there's a lot of trash.

3. (your cat)
   A: _____?
   B: She's small and completely white.

Communication | explain your preference for a vacation destination

4 **Pair Work** Discuss. Match the photos with the cities. What do you know about each city?

———— Beijing   ———— Rio de Janeiro   ———— Barcelona   ———— Mexico City   ———— Las Vegas

5 ▶1.39 Listen to two people deciding where to go on vacation. Which city do they choose? Why?

6 **Group Work** Imagine you have a one-week vacation in March.

1. First, decide which city in the photos you'd like to go to.
   Think about why you want to go there and why you don't want to go to the other cities.

	Barcelona	Mexico City	Beijing	Rio de Janeiro	Las Vegas
Daytime temperature (March)	12 °C/54 °F	17 °C/63 °F	6 °C/43 °F	26 °C/79 °F	13 °C/56 °F
One night's stay	$160	$106	$109	$192	$85
Famous for . . .	🌳 Ⓜ ≈ 🚶	🏛 🛍 🚶 Ⓜ	🏰 🛍 Ⓜ 🏛	≈ 🛍 🚶 🎵	🚶 🛍 🎵
Not famous for . . .	🏛			Ⓜ	🏰 Ⓜ

🌳 parks
Ⓜ art galleries/ museums
≈ beaches
🚶 nightlife
🛍 shopping/markets
🏰 palaces and castles
☕ cafés
🎵 music
🏛 ancient sites

2. As a group, decide on one city to visit. Try to convince other students that your choice is best. Tell them why you decided not to go to the other cities.

> *Wouldn't you guys like to go to Barcelona? I hear it's one of the most interesting cities in Europe.*

> *Don't you think it's a little too far?*

Unit 6 Reference

will: predictions

Use *will* (+ verb) to make predictions about the future.

＋	I/You He/She/It We/They	will	go.
➖	I/You He/She/It We/They	won't	go.
❓	Will	I/you he/she/it we/they	go?
	Yes, I will./No, I won't.		

I (don't) think and *I hope* are often used with *will* when making predictions.

> **I think** the Tigers will win the Cup.
> **I hope** it'll be sunny tomorrow.

Use *I don't think he'll . . .* NOT ~~I think he won't . . .~~

Uses of *like*

Like has different meanings, depending on the grammar of the sentence.

1. *like* = enjoy something in general
   Use *like* + gerund or infinitive.

   A: *What do you* **like to do** *on weekends?*
   B: *I* **like going** *to the mountains.*

2. *would like* = want something or want to do something
   Use *would like* + infinitive or a noun

   A: *What* **would** *you* **like to do** *this weekend?*
   B: *I'd* **like to see** *The Lord of the Rings.*
   C: *I'd* **like a** *quiet* **night** *at home.*

3. *be like* = asking about character or characteristics
   Don't use *like* in the answer.

   A: *What* **is** *your town* **like**?
   B: *It's big and very busy.*

4. *look like* = asking about appearance
   Don't use *like* in the answer.

   A: *What does your father* **look like**?
   B: *He's tall and he has black hair.*

adverbs: *too, too much/many, enough*

Use *too* or *not enough* when something is a problem.

> *His suitcase was* **too heavy** *to carry.*
> *He* **wasn't strong enough** *to carry his suitcase.*

too	Use *too* with adjectives. *I went to bed* **too late** *last night.*
too much	Use *too much* with non-count nouns. *There's* **too much noise** *in here.*
too many	Use *too many* with count nouns. *There are* **too many books** *on that shelf.*
enough	Use *enough* after adjectives and adverbs. Use enough before nouns. *That bag isn't* **big enough**. *He didn't play* **well enough**. *Sorry, I didn't have* **enough time**.

Use *very* when something is difficult but not impossible.

> *His suitcase was* **very** *heavy, but he carried it.*

Unit Vocabulary

Countries and nationalities

Australia/Australian	Brazil/Brazilian
Britain/British	Canada/Canadian
China/Chinese	France/French
Germany/German	Italy/Italian
Japan/Japanese	Kenya/Kenyan
Mexico/Mexican	Spain/Spanish
the United States/American	

Geographical features

sea	beach	island	lake	mountain
river	ocean	forest	desert	

Machines at homes

dishwasher	stove	
MP3 player	hairdryer	vacuum cleaner

UNIT 7
Mind and body

A

B

C

D

Warm Up

1 **Pair Work** Describe the people in the pictures.

> *The man in photo A is in shape.*

2a Check that you understand the meaning of the <u>underlined</u> phrases below.

1. Most men don't spend enough time on their <u>physical appearance</u>.
2. Most women <u>look like</u> their mothers, and most men look like their fathers.
3. It's normal to <u>put on weight</u> as you get older.
4. <u>Going on a diet</u> is bad for your health.
5. You can learn about someone's <u>personality</u> by studying his or her face.
6. Small, everyday things can make people very <u>stressed</u>.

b **Pair Work** Discuss the statements above. Do you agree or disagree?

> *I actually disagree. I think men spend a lot of time on their appearance.*

Reading and Speaking

1 **Group Work** Discuss.

1. Do you read any "celebrity" magazines or watch TV shows about celebrities? Why or why not?

2. Who is the woman in the photos? What do you know about her?

3. Do you think she looks different in the two photos? Why?

2 **Pair Work** Read the article and then take turns asking and answering the questions below.

The perfect body

Most people were surprised when Renée Zellweger got the part of Bridget in the 2001 movie *Bridget Jones's Diary*. The movie is about a young woman who worries about work, her weight, and men. Zellweger is a slim American woman—completely different from Bridget, who is English and overweight.

So what did Zellweger do to get the part right? She had lessons to improve her English accent and she put on about 24 pounds (11 kilos). For several months she didn't do any exercise and she ate a lot of pizza, peanut butter sandwiches, and chocolate. Although it was fun at first, she often felt very sick.

Zellweger put the weight on because she thought it was important to be as real as possible. She was surprised, however, by people's criticisms. People criticized her for being fat when she put on weight for the film. Then they criticized her again for being too skinny when she lost weight after the film. She realized it's almost impossible to have the perfect body in the eyes of the media.

So why did she do it? Well, money was probably one reason. On top of her $15 million salary, she earned $225,000 for every 2.2 pounds (1 kilo) she put on. That's an extra $2.5 million! And it didn't stop there. A British diet magazine paid her $3.5 million to lose all the weight again. So perhaps Zellweger doesn't need to care about the criticism when she earns all this money!

1. Why were people surprised that Renée Zellweger was playing Bridget Jones?
2. How did she put on weight?
3. Why did Zellweger come to believe that "it's almost impossible to have the perfect body in the eyes of the media"?
4. How much did she make in total by putting on and taking off weight?

3 **Pair Work** Read these opinions. Which one(s) do you agree with and why?

a. (People worry too much about weight.) b. (Putting on 24 pounds is dangerous.)

c. (I would do the same in her situation.)

Vocabulary | appearance

4a ▶2.02 Look at the pictures. Listen to two people playing "Guess who . . . ?" Which two people are they describing?

A   B  C   D   E   F

b Pair Work Describe people you know. Use words from the How To box.

c Play "Guess who . . . ?" with a partner, using the pictures above.

Grammar | real conditional

5 ▶2.03 Listen and answer the questions.

1. What product is the ad for?

2. Is the product for men, women, or both?

How To:

Modify adjectives	
With positive adjectives	He's **very/really** good-looking.
	He's **pretty/fairly** muscular.
With negative adjectives	She's **very/really** skinny.
	He's **a little bit/slightly** overweight.
With comparative adjectives	She's **much/a lot** more attractive than most.
	She's **a little bit/slightly** taller than average.

6 Circle the correct <u>underlined</u> choice for each rule in the Active Grammar box.

Active Grammar

1. The real conditional talks about a <u>possible</u> / <u>impossible</u> situation in the future.

   If you use the cream once a day, you'll have softer skin.

   You'll notice the difference if you use the cream twice a day.

2. Make the real conditional with: *If* + <u>simple present</u> / <u>present continuous</u> and *will/won't* + verb.

3. The "*if* clause" comes <u>first</u> / <u>either first or second</u>.

See Reference page 76

7 Complete the sentences with the correct form of the verbs in parentheses.

1. If you _____ (eat) a lot of junk food, you _____ (put) on weight.

2. You _____ (not/sleep) well tonight if you _____ (drink) all that coffee.

3. If he _____ (not/call) you, what _____ (you/do)?

4. He _____ (not/have) any money left if he _____ (buy) any more DVDs.

5. If you _____ (not/train) now, you _____ (not/be able) to run the race.

6. _____ (you/call) me if your bus _____ (be) late?

8 Pair Work Complete these sentences about you. Then compare your sentences.

1. If I have time tomorrow, . . .

2. If it rains this weekend, . . .

3. If I don't go out this evening, . . .

4. If my English is good enough next year, . . .

Vocabulary | personality

1a Match the adjectives in the box with the underlined phrases in the sentences.

> _____ ambitious _____ reserved _____ hard-working _____ open
>
> _____ organized _____ talkative _____ unreliable _____ sensitive

1. My sister is underlined{easily upset}.
2. People in my family are <u>happy to talk about feelings</u>.
3. Sara's boss <u>makes a lot of lists and plans</u>.
4. Paul <u>works hard</u>.
5. It's disappointing when people <u>don't do what they say they will do</u>.
6. Ruth's parents <u>are easy to talk to and talk a lot</u>.
7. Some men <u>don't talk about feelings or problems</u>.
8. Most people <u>really want to be successful</u>.

b **Pair Work** Test your partner. Say a definition. Your partner says the correct word.

> Someone who's easily upset?   Sensitive.

Pronunciation | choice questions with *or*

2a ▶2.04 Choice questions have a rising and falling intonation. Listen and mark the intonation you hear for each adjective with arrows (↗ or ↘).

1. Are you usually hardworking or lazy?
2. Are you more open or more reserved?
3. Are you usually organized or disorganized?
4. Are you a quiet person or a talkative person?

b **Pair Work** Ask and answer the questions with a partner.

Grammar | gerunds and infinitives

3 Look at the examples in the Active Grammar box. Then circle the correct underlined choice to complete each rule.

Active Grammar

*I really **enjoy** talk**ing** about my feelings.*

*I **want to look** at your photo album.*

1. Some verbs are followed by a <u>gerund</u> / <u>infinitive</u> (*enjoy, avoid, miss, finish, consider,* etc.).

2. Some verbs are followed by a <u>gerund</u> / <u>infinitive</u> (*want, seem, offer, decide, hope, afford, promise,* etc.).

See Reference page 76

4a Circle the correct form.

1. He **offered** _to read/reading_ my palm.
2. I've **decided** _not to be/not being_ so lazy.
3. I'm **considering** _to learn/learning_ German.
4. Have you **finished** _to write/writing_ your essay?
5. She's **hoping** _to be/being_ a manager soon.
6. I can't **afford** _to go/going_ to that restaurant.
7. She **promised** _not to be/not being_ late.
8. Carol **missed** _to see/seeing_ Megan.

b **Pair Work** Complete these sentences about your partner. Don't ask him or her, just guess.

1. He or she really wants _____ after the lesson.
2. He or she's decided _____ for his or her next vacation.
3. He or she really enjoys _____ on weekends.
4. He or she usually avoids _____ because he or she doesn't like it.
5. He or she's considering _____ next year.

c Say your sentences to your partner and find out if they are true or not.

Reading and Speaking

5a Read the information below and decide what type of hands you have.

TEXTURE OF HANDS

Soft Hands

Soft hands can mean that the person is calm but sometimes rather lazy. They are often not very ambitious.

Hard Hands

People with hard hands sometimes get angry easily. They are often very ambitious and energetic.

SHAPE OF HANDS

Point Hands

This can mean the person is artistic, sensitive, and kind. Often these people work with fashion or hairdressing.

Square Hands

People with square hands are usually hard working, organized, and reliable. They are often good with money and business.

b **Pair Work** Tell your partner about his or her personality, using the vocabulary words from Exercise 1a and the text above. Talk about the texture and shape of his or her hands.

c **Group Work** Discuss. How accurate do you think the information is?

Listening

1 **Pair Work** Look at the "*Doctor, doctor*" jokes and discuss the questions.

1. Do you think they are funny?
2. Do you have "*Doctor, doctor*" jokes like this in your language?

2 ▶2.05 Listen to two friends telling "*Doctor, doctor*" jokes. What's the "problem" in each one?

3 **Pair Work** Do you know any other jokes? Tell your jokes and respond to your partner's jokes. Use the sentences in the How To box below.

How To:		
Respond to jokes		
😆	*That's really funny!*	🙂 *I don't get it.*
🙂	*That's pretty funny.*	😐 *That's not very funny.*

Vocabulary | illness and injury

4a Complete the chart using these words and phrases.

the flu	a headache	a broken arm/leg	food poisoning	a backache
a cold	an earache	a pain in my chest	a stomach ache	
a fever	feel sick	a sore throat	a toothache	

Illness	Injury	Symptom

b We say "feel" sick. What verb do we use for all the other phrases?

c ▶2.06 Listen and check your answers.

5 **Pair Work** Take turns matching these suggestions with the correct symptoms in Exercise 4a.

Ex: You should go to the *dentist.*  toothache

1. You should put a cold wet cloth on your forehead.
2. You should sleep on a firm mattress.
3. Have you tried sucking on a cough drop?
4. Have you tried taking an aspirin?

6a ▶2.07 **Pair Work** Listen. Then practice the conversation with a partner.

A: I have a sore throat.
B: Oh, I'm sorry. You should drink some tea.
A: Good idea.

b Practice similar conversations with your partner, using the phrases from Exercise 4a.

Grammar | reasons/purpose: *because/so that/in order to*

7 Read the letter below. What do you think Rick's problem was?

> *Dear Rick,*
>
> *Thanks for your letter. This is a common problem <u>because people don't stand</u>[1] or sit in the right way. There are lots of things you can do to help. First, make sure you get the right chair <u>to support</u>[2] your back. Second, think about changing your mattress. You should sleep on a firm mattress <u>in order to keep</u>[3] your back straight during the night.*
>
> *You should also take regular breaks <u>so that you change</u>[4] your sitting position. You should exercise every day, too. <u>In order not to make</u>[5] your back worse, don't go running. Go swimming or do yoga instead.*
>
> *Good luck!*
> *Doctor Darren*

8 Look at the <u>underlined</u> phrases in the letter. Write the number of a phrase that illustrates each rule in the Active Grammar box

Writing

9a Write a short letter to Doctor Darren asking for advice about a problem.

b **Pair Work** Read your partner's letter. You are Doctor Darren. Write a reply giving advice.

c Read your partner's reply. Do you think he or she gave you good advice?

Active Grammar

1. Giving a reason:
   _____ *because* + subject + verb

2. Expressing a purpose:
   a. _____ *so (that)* + subject + verb
   b. _____ infinitive
   c. _____ *in order (not) to* + base form

See Reference page 76

Extra Listening Activity
in ACTIVEBOOK

Review

1   Write real conditional sentences using the cues.

Ex: she/eat all that cake/have a stomach ache

_If she eats all that cake, she'll have a stomach ache_____.

1. they/offer me the job/take it   _____.
2. I/not study/not pass my test   _____.
3. you/not use suntan lotion/get a sunburn   _____.
4. I/be late for work/not get up now   _____.
5. we/not invite her/she be upset   _____.
6. we/not leave now/be late   _____.

2   Choose the correct alternatives.

Ex: I expect _passing/(to pass)_ my driving test.

1. I enjoy _going/to go_ to the movies.
2. I promise _not telling/not to tell_ anyone.
3. He offered _washing/to wash_ the dishes.
4. I considered _taking/to take_ a computer course.
5. She's decided _going/to go_ running every day.
6. They miss _living/to live_ with their parents.
7. I hope _seeing/to see_ you soon.
8. He avoided _talking/to talk_ to his girlfriend.

3   Complete the sentences with the gerund or infinitive form of the verbs in parentheses.

Ex: We've decided _to eat_____ (eat) at home this evening.

1. I'm considering _____ (go) to Thailand for my next vacation.
2. I'm hoping _____ (lose) about four pounds by the end of March.
3. Gabriela offered _____ (help) me with my homework.
4. We'll leave early to avoid _____ (arrive) after dark.
5. I want _____ (do) a lot of work this weekend.
6. Let me know when you've finished _____ (talk) on the phone.

4   Choose the correct alternatives.

Ex: I'm getting a new computer _(so that)/to_ I can work at home.

1. I'm going to bed now _so/because_ I'm very tired.
2. She always walks to work _to/so that_ keep fit.
3. I always write lists _because/so that_ I don't forget anything.
4. My car broke down, _so/in order to_ I was late for the party.
5. I use an alarm clock _in order not to/so that_ wake up late.
6. He always buys theater tickets early _because/to_ get good seats.

Communication |
understand and talk about a magazine quiz

5 **Pair Work** Discuss.

1. Are you someone who gets stressed easily?

2. What things make you stressed?

6a **Pair Work** Take the stress quiz with a partner.

b Add up your Total Stress Factor. Then find out what it means on page 131.

c How accurate do you think the Total Stress Factor results are for you?

7 **Group Work** Discuss.

1. Which of the following things do you do to relax?

> watch TV do yoga
> take a bath sing
> talk to a friend
> play a physically hard sport
> play computer games
> listen to music
> get a massage
> close your eyes and
>   breathe deeply

2. What other things do you do?

QUIZ
Stress?
What stress?

For each situation, write your Stress Factor (1–5).

1 No problem
2 Not happy, but keeping cool
3 Getting a little tense
4 Heart is beating faster
5 Major stress alert

❶ You wait for a bus for 20 minutes. When the bus comes, you can't get on because there are too many people on it. **Stress Factor:** ____

❷ You walk to work. It starts raining heavily and you don't have an umbrella. You get completely soaked. **Stress Factor:** ____

❸ You take some clothes back to a store. The sales clerk won't give your money back because you've lost the receipt. **Stress Factor:** ____

❹ You call a customer service line to try and fix your computer. You don't get to speak to a person, just a machine. **Stress Factor:** ____

❺ You're in your car at a traffic light. Another driver shouts at you for not moving quickly enough. **Stress Factor:** ____

❻ You go to a theater to see a really good movie. Some people next to you won't stop talking and eating loudly. **Stress Factor:** ____

❼ You play a game of tennis with a friend. You don't play well and he or she beats you easily. **Stress Factor:** ____

❽ You're just about to go to work or school. You realize you can't find an important document or piece of homework. **Stress Factor:** ____

❾ You're in bed and you can't sleep because the dog next door is barking. **Stress Factor:** ____

❿ You want to pay for something, but the store clerk is talking on the phone and not looking at you. **Stress Factor:** ____

Unit 7 Reference

Real conditional

Use the real conditional to talk about a possible situation in the future.

If + simple present, *will* + verb

Don't use *will* in the "*if* clause."

> *If we leave at 9:30, we'll be late.*

> NOT: ~~*If we'll leave at 9:30, we'll be late.*~~

The "*if* clause" can come first or second.

When the "*if* clause" is first, put a comma at the end of the clause.

> *If I don't go to bed now, I'll be too tired tomorrow.*
> *He'll fail his exam if he doesn't work harder.*

Other modal verbs can also be used in the "result" clause (not just *will*). Ex: *may, might, could*.

> *If I finish this soon, I might go and see Tony.*
> *Bobby may bring his son if he comes on Sunday.*

Other time words (with a present tense) can also be used to talk about the future. Ex: *when, as soon as.*

> *When I see him, I'll tell him.*
> *As soon as he arrives, we'll have dinner.*

Gerunds and infinitives

Some verbs are followed by a gerund and some are followed by an infinitive.

Verbs followed by a gerund include:
enjoy, avoid, imagine, consider, finish, miss

> *I enjoy playing tennis.*
> *I can't imagine going to the moon.*
> *Would you consider working part time?*

Verbs followed by an infinitive include:
want, seem, offer, decide, hope, afford, expect, promise

> *I want to see that new movie.*
> *He decided to take piano lessons.*
> *I'm hoping to go to college next year.*

Reason/purpose

Expressing purpose
Use these structures to express purpose:

to + verb
in order (not) to + verb
so that + subject + verb

In order to is more formal than *to* and *so that*.

> *I'm writing to you in order to complain about the meal.*
> *I'd like to talk to the manager to explain the problem.*
> *I have a bottle of water with me so that I don't get thirsty.*

Giving a reason
Use *because* + subject + verb to give reasons:

> *I'm studying very hard because I have my exams in two weeks.*

Unit Vocabulary

Describing appearance
tall	attractive	overweight
short	muscular	good-looking
skinny	handsome	

Describing character
open	talkative	organized
sensitive	unreliable	hard-working
reserved	ambitious	

Illnesses and injuries
flu	food poisoning
a cold	a broken arm or leg

Symptoms
feel sick	a sore throat
an earache	a stomach ache
a headache	a pain in my chest
a backache	a fever
a toothache	

UNIT 8
Life in the fast lane

Warm Up

1 **Group Work** Look at the photos. What can you see? What is the connection?

2a Check you understand the meanings of the underlined phrases.
  1. Are you the type of person who is always in a hurry?
  2. Do you usually arrive on time for things? How do you feel if you're late?
  3. What time is rush hour in your town? What is it like?
  4. Do you usually speed up or slow down when the traffic light is yellow? Why?
  5. Do you think speed cameras on roads are a good idea? Why or why not?

b **Pair Work** Ask and answer the questions with a partner. Which of you lives a "faster" life?

LESSON 1
Describe simple changes
GRAMMAR passive voice: present

Reading

1a Read the website *Fast Foods with Slow Tips*.

Food

FAST FACTS: Sixty-five million fast-food meals are eaten in the US every day.

In 1970, Americans spent about $6 billion on fast food. They now spend more than $110 billion a year, and this figure continues to rise.

In 1968, McDonald's had about 1,000 restaurants. Today it has about 33,000 around the world, and this number goes up by almost 2,000 each year.

SLOW TIPS: Make your own food. It's tastier, better for you, and you'll enjoy doing it. Sit down and eat with other people. Don't eat "on the go" or at your desk.

Communication

FAST FACTS: Over 2.5 billion text messages are sent each day in the US.

An average office worker checks email 50 times a day, deals with over 150 emails, and sends or receives over 70 text messages every day.

SLOW TIPS: Write one long email instead of three short ones.

Turn your cell phone off or leave it at home sometimes.

Travel

FAST FACTS: Over 400 million cars are currently used around the world.

London rush-hour traffic moves at an average of thirteen kilometers (eight miles) per hour.

Two out of three people speed up when the traffic light turns yellow.

SLOW TIPS: Leave your car at home if you can and walk. Your fitness will improve, and you'll probably get there more quickly.

Spend at least 20 minutes a day in a garden or park. Sit, think, look at the trees, talk, read, enjoy the sky.

b Correct the sentences.

> **Ex:** The amount of money spent on fast food in the US is going ~~down~~. *up*

1. The website recommends having lunch in front of your computer.
2. Americans send more than 2.5 million emails every day.
3. The website says you should have your phone with you all the time.
4. The maximum speed of cars in London's rush hour is 13 kilometers an hour.
5. Most people slow down when the traffic light turns yellow.
6. The website says driving in a city is probably quicker than walking.
7. The website suggests relaxing at home for 20 minutes each day.

2 **Pair Work** Look again at the "Slow Tips" from the website and discuss with a partner:

1. Do you do the things they suggest? Do you think they are good ideas? Why or why not?

> *I live by myself, so I don't make my own food very often. But . . .*

2. Discuss one more tip for each section. Tell other students your tips.

> *I think it's important to eat a lot of fresh fruits and vegetables.*

Grammar | passive voice: present

3 Look at the examples in the Active Grammar box and circle the correct choices to complete the rules.

> ### Active Grammar
>
> 1. Most sentences in English are in the **active voice**.
>   Form: <u>subject</u> / <u>object</u> + verb + <u>subject</u> / <u>object</u>
>   *Americans spend more than $110 billion on fast food every year.*
>
> 2. Use the **passive voice** when who or what causes the action is unknown or not important.
>   Form: *am, is,* or *are* + <u>infinitive</u> / <u>past participle</u>
>   *Sixty-five million fast-food meals **are eaten** every day in the US.*

See Reference page 86

4 Complete the sentences with a verb from the box in the passive voice.

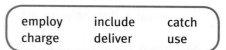

| employ | include | catch |
| charge | deliver | use |

1. Pizzas _____ in 20 minutes or you get your money back.
2. Service _____ in the bill.
3. Many drivers _____ by speed cameras.
4. The subways _____ by thousands of people every day.
5. Millions of people _____ in the fast-food industry.
6. Customers _____ 36 yen per minute to eat in the Totenko restaurant in Tokyo.

Vocabulary | verbs about change

5a Circle the correct word or phrase to complete each sentence.

1. The number of fast-food restaurants is *going up/getting better* steadily.
2. The quality of food that most people eat has *gotten worse/fallen* recently.
3. The amount of traffic has *increased/improved* over the last few years.
4. The air quality in most cities is *deteriorating/going down* rapidly.

b ▶2.08 Listen and check your answers.

Speaking

6 **Pair Work** Talk about the changes in your area or country. Use the ideas below and language from the How To box.

> quality of restaurants
> number of fast-food restaurants
> wages   air quality   traffic

How To:	
Talk about simple changes	
What change?	*Prices have gone up . . .* *Air quality has deteriorated . . .*
How fast?	*. . . dramatically . . .* *. . . steadily . . .* *. . . slightly . . .*
When?	*. . . recently.* *. . . in the last two years.* *. . . since 2010.*

Vocabulary | phrasal verbs—relationships

1 Write the phrasal verbs in the questions below next to their correct definitions.

_____ a. date

_____ b. stop being someone's partner

_____ c. slowly stop having a good relationship

ask someone out d. invite someone to

_____ e. stop feeling sad about

_____ f. accept a bad situation without complaining

1. Do women ever <u>ask</u> men <u>out</u> in your country?

2. What do you think is the minimum time you should <u>go out with</u> someone before you get married?

3. Do you think couples who marry young often <u>grow apart</u>? Why or why not?

4. If your partner never did household chores, would you <u>put up with</u> it? Why or why not?

5. For what reasons do people usually <u>break up with</u> their partner?

6. What different ways do people use to <u>get over</u> the end of a relationship?

2 **Pair Work** Discuss the questions in Exercise 1.

Reading

3a Look at the photo and scorecard. What do you think "speed-dating" is?

b Read the letter.

SpeedDate

Dear Rachel,

Thank you for reserving a spot at our next speed-dating event.

What to expect:
Speed-dating is a fast way to meet a new partner. There are 20 men and 20 women, and you have *just three minutes* to talk to each person. After three minutes, if you like the person, put a check by his or her name on your score card. Then move on and talk to the next person. At the end, give us your score card. If you checked someone who also checked you, we will give you each other's email addresses.

A few tips:
Don't start every conversation with "What do you do?" This gets pretty boring. And don't ask too many *yes/no* questions. Ask interesting questions, like "How would your best friend describe you?" or "What was the last song you downloaded?"

When?
Saturday, January 16th. Arrive at 7.00 P.M.

Where?
Studio 44, 44 Ashton Street

Happy dating!

Julia Jones

Manager

Speed Date Scorecard			
Your name: Ken Clark			
Number:	Name:	Yes (✓)	Comments:
12	Anna		Too serious
13	Wendy	✓	Funny and interesting
14	Tara		

4 Look back at the letter and answer the questions.

1. How many people are there at this event?
2. How long do you get to speak to each person?
3. What should you do with your card?
4. Whose email addresses will you get?
5. What types of questions shouldn't you ask?
6. What questions should you ask?

5 **Group Work** Discuss.

1. What do you think about speed-dating?
2. Do you think it might be a good way to meet someone?

Listening

6a ▶2.09 Listen to two conversations at a speed-dating event. Which pair followed the advice in the letter?

_____ Melanie and Steve   _____ Rachel and Kieron

b Listen again and write the initial of the person (Melanie, Steve, Rachel, or Kieron) who:

_____ 1. is a teacher.
_____ 2. is an architect.
_____ 3. likes his or her job.
_____ 4. has never done speed-dating before.
_____ 5. is friendly.
_____ 6. has a teach-yourself-Italian CD.
_____ 7. loves Italy.

Grammar | review of question types

7 Read the Active Grammar box and fill in the blanks with *Yes/No* or *Information*.

> ### Active Grammar
>
> These are two main types of questions:
>
> 1. _____ questions: *Do you enjoy your job?*
> 2. _____ questions: *How would your best friend describe you?*

See Reference page 86

8 **Pair Work** With a partner, think of six interesting questions to ask someone at a speed-dating event.

Pronunciation | rising and falling intonation

9 Practice saying your questions from Exercise 8. Use rising intonation for *yes/no* questions. Use falling intonation for information questions.

Speaking

10 **Group Work** Imagine you are at a party. Talk to other students and find out some interesting information about each person. You only have two minutes with each person.

Ask and answer questions about past actions

GRAMMAR past continuous and simple past

Reading

1   Read the three jokes below. Then
     answer the questions.

1

A man was speeding down a highway
surrounded by cars all going around 80 miles
an hour. While he was passing another car, an
officer with a radar gun pulled him over. When
the officer was handing the man the ticket, the
man complained, "I know I was speeding, but
this isn't fair. All the other cars around me were
speeding, too." The officer asked, "Have you
ever gone fishing?" The man answered that he
had. The officer said, "Have you ever caught
ALL the fish?"

2

An officer pulled a young woman over for doing 50 mph
in a 35 mph zone. As the officer was writing the ticket, he
asked the woman why she was going so fast. "I wanted to
get there before I got lost," she replied.

3

A car was driving very slowly down a highway when an officer stopped
it. Inside were four elderly women. The officer told the driver that she
was going too slowly. "But officer," she said, "I was going 22 miles per
hour—exactly the speed posted on the sign." The officer smiled and
said, "Ma'am, this is Highway 22. The speed limit is 60." He looked at
the other women, who all looked very frightened. "Are they OK?" The
officer asked. The driver said, "Well, we just got off of Highway 150."

150 mph = 241.4 km/h

1. How did the officer catch the man in the first joke?
2. Why did the man protest the ticket?
3. What did the officer mean when he said, "Have you ever caught ALL the fish?"
4. In the second joke, what reason did the woman give for speeding?
5. Why did the officer stop the car in the third joke?
6. Why was the woman going 22 miles an hour?
7. Why were the other women in the car frightened?

2   **Pair Work** Discuss.
1. What is the "punch line," or funniest sentence, in each joke?
2. What makes each joke funny?
3. Which joke do you think is the funniest? Why?
4. Have you or has anyone you know been given a speeding ticket? What happened?

Grammar | past continuous and simple past

3 Complete the Active Grammar box by writing *simple past* or *past continuous*.

> **Active Grammar**
>
> 1. Use the _____ to talk about an action in progress at a particular time in the past.
>   *A man and a woman were speeding down a highway.*
> 2. Use the _____ to talk about completed actions in the past.
>   *An officer pulled a young woman over.*
> 3. Use the _____ to talk about an action in progress interrupted by another action.
>   *A car was driving very slowly down a highway when an officer stopped it.*

See Reference page 86

4 Complete the sentences using the simple past or the past continuous of the verbs in parentheses.

1. I _____ (walk) home when I _____ (meet) Sarah.
2. Pablo _____ (take) a photo of me when I _____ (not/look).
3. I _____ (read) a magazine when the train _____ (arrive).
4. How fast _____ (you drive) when the accident _____ (happen)?

5 Complete the sentences. Use the simple past or the past continuous.

1. I cut my finger while I _____.
2. I was playing the piano when my friend _____.
3. Maki broke her leg while she _____.
4. When I was living in France, I _____.

Speaking

6a **SPEAKING EXCHANGE** Work in groups of four—two As and two Bs.

> **Students A:** Follow the directions on page 127.
> **Students B:** Follow the directions on page 131.

b Report back. Did Students A commit the crime?

Writing

7 Read the story in the Writing bank on page 135. Do the exercises.

8 Write a story starting with the following words:

It all happened last summer . . .

Review

1 Complete the sentences with the passive form of the verbs in the box.

> **Ex:** Cheese __*is made*__ from milk.

cover	cut down
invite	serve
lock	clean
~~make~~	employ

1. The rooms in this hotel _____ at 10:00 every morning.
2. You _____ to Paul and Sheila's wedding.
3. Thousands of trees _____ every year.
4. Most of the Earth's surface _____ by water.
5. The park gates _____ at 6:00 P.M.
6. Breakfast _____ from 7:00 to 9:00.
7. Many people _____ by the city government.

2 Write the questions. Then take turns asking and answering.

> **Ex:** My favorite drink is . . .
>
> What __*is your favorite drink*_____?

1. I like eating . . . for breakfast.
   What _____?
2. I can . . . really well.
   What _____?
3. I'm going to go on vacation in . . .
   When _____?

3 Complete the paragraphs with the past continuous or simple past form of the verbs in parentheses.

> At about 6:30 yesterday evening, I __*was riding*_____ (ride) my bike home from work. It _____ (1. rain), and a lot of people _____ (2. drive) too fast. Suddenly, a car _____ (3. stop) in front of me. I _____ (4. not hit) the car, but I _____ (5. fall) off my bicycle. Luckily, I _____ (6. not be) hurt.
>
> A couple of years ago, I _____ (7. walk) home along a dark street. Somebody _____ (8. follow) me and I was very frightened. I _____ (9. start) to run, but when I _____ (10. look) back, I _____ (11. see) my friend Daniel. I was so glad!

4 Replace the underlined word in each sentence with the correct word.

> **Ex:** I really like him. I hope he asks me ~~up~~ *out* soon.

1. Sophia's had the flu for three days, but she's <u>going</u> over it now.
2. You must slow <u>up</u>—the lights are turning red.
3. Tom's so lazy! Why do you put <u>on</u> with it?
4. I never drive into the city during rush <u>time</u>.
5. Why don't you relax? You're always <u>at</u> a hurry.
6. Lian and I were best friends in high school. We've grown <u>away</u> now.

Communication | talk for an extended period on a familiar topic

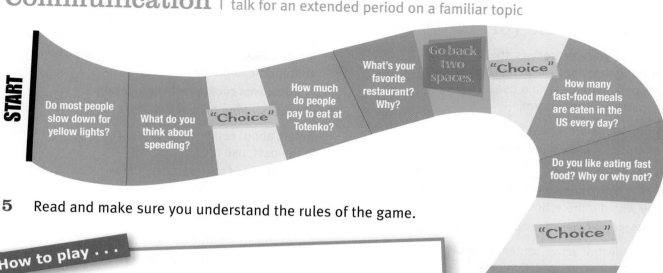

START

Do most people slow down for yellow lights?

What do you think about speeding?

"Choice"

How much do people pay to eat at Totenko?

What's your favorite restaurant? Why?

Go back two spaces.

"Choice"

How many fast-food meals are eaten in the US every day?

Do you like eating fast food? Why or why not?

5 Read and make sure you understand the rules of the game.

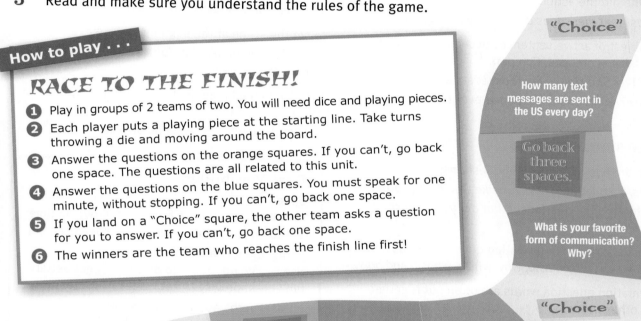

How to play . . .

RACE TO THE FINISH!

1 Play in groups of 2 teams of two. You will need dice and playing pieces.

2 Each player puts a playing piece at the starting line. Take turns throwing a die and moving around the board.

3 Answer the questions on the orange squares. If you can't, go back one space. The questions are all related to this unit.

4 Answer the questions on the blue squares. You must speak for one minute, without stopping. If you can't, go back one space.

5 If you land on a "Choice" square, the other team asks a question for you to answer. If you can't, go back one space.

6 The winners are the team who reaches the finish line first!

"Choice"

How many text messages are sent in the US every day?

Go back three spaces.

What is your favorite form of communication? Why?

"Choice"

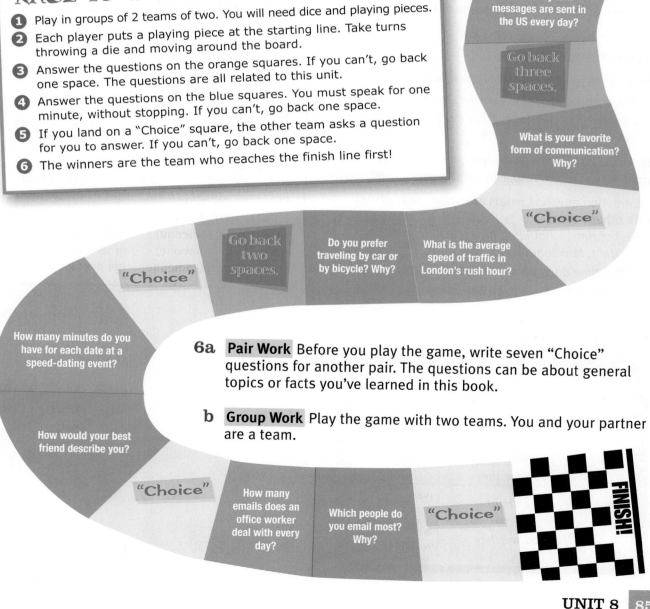

"Choice"

Go back two spaces.

Do you prefer traveling by car or by bicycle? Why?

What is the average speed of traffic in London's rush hour?

How many minutes do you have for each date at a speed-dating event?

How would your best friend describe you?

"Choice"

How many emails does an office worker deal with every day?

Which people do you email most? Why?

"Choice"

FINISH!

6a **Pair Work** Before you play the game, write seven "Choice" questions for another pair. The questions can be about general topics or facts you've learned in this book.

b **Group Work** Play the game with two teams. You and your partner are a team.

Unit 8 Reference

Passive voice (present)

In active voice sentences, the subject is the person or thing that does the action. Use the passive when the person or thing who does the action is not important or not known.

Form: *am/is/are* + past participle
*Most computers **are made** in Asia.*

The passive voice is also used when the object of the active voice sentence is the main focus. Use *by* to say who did the action.

*Most text messages are sent **by teenagers**.*

The object of active sentences becomes the subject of passive sentences. Compare:

Active: *She cleans **my room** every day.*
Passive: ***My room** is cleaned every day.*

Question types

There are two main types of questions:

Yes/No questions: *Do you like watching football?*
Information questions: *What did you do last weekend?*

The most common information question words are: *what, where, when, who, why, which, whose,* and *how.*

Information question words are often put together with other words:
Ex: *what time, what kind, how much, how many, how often, how long, which one.*

***What time** does your train leave?*
***How long** have you lived here?*

Past continuous

⊕ ⊖	I/He/She/It	was wasn't	waiting . . .
	You/We/They	were weren't	
?	Was	I/he/she/it	eating . . .
	Were	you/we/they	
	Yes, No,	I/he/she/it	was. wasn't.
	Yes, No,	you/we/they	were. weren't.

Use the past continuous to talk about an action or situation that was in progress at a particular time in the past. Past continuous actions are not complete at that time in the past.

*Adam **was cooking** when I got home.*
*I **was waiting** for the bus at six thirty.*

To talk about completed actions at a particular time in the past, use the simple past.

*I **sent** David a present yesterday.*
*Martin **cooked** dinner last night.*

The past continuous is often used

to set the scene at the beginning of a story.

It was raining heavily. Julia was walking quickly toward the theater.

to talk about a longer action interrupted by another action.

I was watching TV when he arrived.

Unit Vocabulary

Speed

rush hour	be in a hurry	arrive on time
speed up	slow down	speed camera

Verbs about change

rise	go up	go down	get better
fall	improve	get worse	deteriorate

Phrasal verbs about relationships

go out with (someone)	ask someone out
put up with (someone)	grow apart
break up with (someone)	get over (someone)

UNIT 9
Careers

A

B

C

D

Warm Up

1 Group Work What jobs do you see in the pictures? Find out what jobs three classmates do. If you don't know what a job is, ask the student to explain.

2a Group Work Number the phrases below in a logical order (1–9).

> I think you have to prepare a resumé first . . .

_____ get promoted	_____ have an interview
_____ apply for a job	_1_ prepare a resumé
_____ work long hours	_____ run your own company
_____ be offered a job	_____ take a job _____ resign

b Pair Work Which of the things have you done? Tell another student about your experiences.

Vocabulary | work

1a What is the difference in meaning between each pair of words?

1. an employer/an employee
2. an interviewer/an interviewee
3. an application form/a resumé
4. experience/education

5. a salary/a bonus
6. a receptionist/a secretary
7. a company/a factory
8. a managing director/a sales rep

b Circle the correct choice to complete each sentence.

1. Most of our *employers/employees* have been with the company since it opened last year.
2. A good *managing director/sales rep* knows how to listen to people and give them the products they need.
3. I'm afraid we need someone for this job with much more *experience/education*.
4. It's very important that a *receptionist/secretary* is welcoming to visitors.
5. If we reach our sales targets, we will get a 20 percent *salary/bonus*.
6. A good *interviewer/interviewee* knows how to ask the right questions.
7. I must fill out the *application form/resumé* for that job at CoffeeCo today.

Pronunciation | word stress

2a ▶2.10 Listen and mark the main stress on each word or phrase in Exercise 1a.

Ex: an empl<u>o</u>yer/an employ<u>ee</u>

b **Pair Work** Say each word or phrase to your partner.

3 Discuss these questions.

1. What qualities make a good interviewer/secretary/sales rep/managing director?
2. What information should you include in a resumé? What order should it be in?
3. What is a typical salary in your country for a secretary/a sales rep?
4. Would you rather have a high salary and no bonus, or an average salary and possible bonuses?
5. When was the last time you were an interviewee? How did you feel?

Reading

4 **Pair Work** Read the article. Then take turns asking and answering the questions below.

HOW TO GET THAT JOB!

Before the interview

- Find out as much as you can about the company.
- Think about questions that the interviewer might ask you. Plan your answers.
- Dress well.
- Don't be late. If you are very early, go to a nearby coffee shop and look at your notes.
- Turn off your cell phone and take two or three slow, deep breaths before you go in.

During the interview

- When you walk in, shake hands firmly with the interviewer, look him or her in the eyes and say,

"Pleased to meet you."
- Answer the questions in a confident, firm voice. Don't speak too quietly or too quickly, or be too hesitant.
- Answers should not be one word or one sentence but also should not be too long.
- When answering questions, maintain eye contact with the interviewer. If there is more than one interviewer, give them equal attention.
- Give clear, direct answers to questions. If you don't know something, say so.
- Don't lie.

- At the end of the interview, you might be asked, "Are there any questions that you would like to ask us?" Make sure you have one or two good questions ready.
- Above all, be positive and show enthusiasm for the job.

After the interview

- Be sure to send a thank-you note promptly. If there was more than one interviewer, send each person a note. Thank them for their time and mention some of the topics from the interview that you would like them to remember. Keep your note polite and to the point.

1. What research do you need to do before the interview?
2. What should you do if you arrive very early?
3. What should you do just before you enter the interview room?
4. What should you do and say when you meet the interviewer?
5. How long should your answers to questions be?
6. How should you answer questions?
7. Where should you look when you answer questions?
8. What should your general attitude in the interview be?
9. What might you do after the interview?

5 **Group Work** Discuss.

1. Do you disagree with any of the points in the article? If so, which ones? Why?
2. Do you think you are good or bad at job interviews? Why?
3. Would you rather work for yourself or work in a company? Why?

Speaking

6 **SPEAKING EXCHANGE** Follow the directions on page 129. Student A is the interviewee. Student B is the interviewer.

Reading

1 **Pair Work** Read the article. Then take turns asking and answering the questions below.

World's Youngest Billionaire

Who is the world's youngest billionaire? Mark Zuckerberg, founder and CEO of Facebook. Born in New York in 1984, he became interested in creating computer programs when he was in high school. Then in 2004, during his second year in college, he created an online directory where all the students at his college <u>could be</u> listed. He launched it from his dorm room and called it "thefacebook.com." A few months later, Zuckerberg dropped out of college to work on the program, and the rest is history. Facebook now has over 500 million users around the world.

What is Zuckerberg's lifestyle like? Although he's worth over $4 billion, he wears sneakers and jeans, lives in a small one-bedroom apartment, and sleeps on a mattress on the floor. He is frequently up working until 6 or 8 A.M. and sometimes doesn't sleep for days. What makes him happy? He <u>is able to do</u> the work that he loves. And he hopes he <u>will be able to continue</u> to build new ways for people to connect in the future. As he says, "The thing I'm most excited about is what we're building now. And I <u>can't talk</u> about that."

1. How old was Zuckerberg when he created Facebook?
2. What was the original purpose of Facebook?
3. Does Zuckerberg have expensive tastes? Explain.
4. What is his work schedule like?
5. What motivates Zuckerberg?
6. What does he hope he will be able to do in the future?

2 **Group Work** Discuss.

1. Would you like to have Zuckerberg's lifestyle and work routine? Why or why not?
2. What are the pros and cons of being a wealthy CEO when you are young?
3. What kind of work do you really love doing? Would you like to be able to devote your life to it?

Grammar | *can, could, be able to*: ability

3 Look at the underlined verb phrases in the reading. Then complete the Active Grammar box with *can/can't, could, is/are able to,* or *will be able to.*

> **Active Grammar**
>
> 1. Use _____ or _____ to talk about ability in the present.
>
> 2. Use _____ or *was/were able to* to talk about ability in the past.
>
> 3. Use _____ to talk about ability in the future.

See Reference page 96

4 Complete the sentences with *can/can't, could/couldn't,* or *able to.*

1. David _____ play the piano quite well now.
2. I wasn't _____ get to sleep last night. I kept thinking about work.
3. I _____ lift this box. It's too heavy.
4. Lan _____ write simple computer programs by the time she was 12.
5. They looked everywhere for Suzie's ring, but they _____ find it.
6. _____ you hear what Pablo was saying? It was very noisy in the restaurant.
7. He'll be _____ speak more fluently if he practices more.

5 **Pair Work** Look at the chart. Take turns saying how well Melissa *could, can,* or *was/is/will be able to* play the guitar, swim, cook, and paint.

XX = not at all   *X* = not very well
✓ = pretty well   ✓✓ = very well

	A	B	C	D
5 years ago	X	XX	✓	XX
Now	✓	XX	✓	X
5 years from now	✓✓	X	✓✓	X

> *Five years ago she couldn't play the guitar very well.*

Speaking

6a **Pair Work** For each activity in Exercise 5, tell another student how well you:

1. could/were able to do it in the past.
2. can/are able to do it now.
3. think you will be able to do it in the future.

b Choose two other activities to describe in the same way.

7a **Pair Work** Discuss the things:

1. you could do one year ago in English.
2. you can do now in English.
3. you want to be able to do a year from now.

b Discuss how you are going to improve. Discuss tasks you can do and when you can do them.

> **Some ideas:**
> Ask for directions
> Talk about your hobbies
> Order a meal in a restaurant
> Give advice about illnesses
> Read newspaper articles

LESSON 3
Write a short article
GRAMMAR passive voice: past

Vocabulary | crime

1 Answer the questions, using the words and phrases in the box.

> judge   thief
> jury   police officer

1. Who **steals** things? _____

2. Who **arrests** criminals? _____

3. Who decides if a **criminal** is **guilty** or **innocent**? _____

4. Who can decide what **punishment** to give a criminal, for example, a **fine** or a **jail sentence**?

_____

Listening

2 ▶ **2.11** Listen to a news story. Mark the sentences true (*T*) or false (*F*).

_____ 1. Mr. Grumbel was sentenced to five years in jail.

_____ 2. He was charged with stealing 39 cars.

_____ 3. The cars were stolen from car dealerships in Texas.

_____ 4. Each of the cars was sprayed with perfume.

_____ 5. The cars were all found outside Mr. Grumbel's house.

_____ 6. Mr. Grumbel liked to pretend he was rich.

_____ 7. He was arrested when he was seen stealing one of the cars.

3 **Pair Work** Discuss.

1. What do you think about Grumbel's punishment? Was it too short or too long? Why?

2. Do you know of any other funny or unusual crimes?

Grammar | passive voice: past

4 Read the Active Grammar box and circle the correct <u>underlined</u> choices.

> ### Active Grammar
>
> 1. Use the <u>active</u> / <u>passive</u> form to say what the subject did.
>   *Grumbel stole new cars.* (Grumbel performed the action)
>
> 2. Use the <u>active</u> / <u>passive</u> to say what happened to the subject. Use it when who or what causes the action is unknown or not important.
>   *Thirty-nine cars were stolen.* (the cars received the action)
>
> Form: *was* or *were* + past participle
>   *I **wasn't given** anything to eat.*
>   *What punishment **were** they **given**?*

See Reference page 96

5 **Pair Work** Find five examples of the passive in the audioscript on page 143.

6 Complete the sentences with a verb from the box. Use the passive voice in the past tense.

> arrest   clean   invent   send   meet

1. All the employees _____ a letter by the CEO.
2. The bicycle _____ over 150 years ago.
3. We _____ at the airport by a tour guide.
4. Two men _____ by the police for stealing $2,000.
5. This carpet _____ last week, and now look at how dirty it is!

7 Circle the correct choices in the story below.

Germany's worst bank robber _gave/was given_ (1) a one-year suspended sentence* after a judge _felt/was felt_ (2) sorry for him. The court _told/was told_ (3) how Marko N., 28, _waited/was waited_ (4) outside the bank for three hours trying to get over his nerves. He then _ran/was run_ (5) into the bank with a wool hat over his face. Unfortunately, he couldn't see anything. He _took/was taken_ (6) off the hat in front of the security camera and demanded money from the cashier. He was holding a cigarette lighter in the shape of a gun. She just _told/was told_ (7) him to go away. Finally, he ran off and _arrested/was arrested_ (8) by the police outside the bank. He _took/was taken_ (9) in a van to the nearest police station. "Give up on being a bank robber," the judge told him. "You have no talent for the job."

> **Glossary**
> * a _suspended sentence_ = you only go to jail if you commit another crime

Speaking

8a Look at the paragraph in Exercise 7. What is the _introduction_, _the story_, and _conclusion_? Use the How To box to help you.

b **SPEAKING EXCHANGE** Work in two groups.

  Group A: Look at the picture story on page 128.
  Group B: Look at the picture story on page 132.
  Work with your group to create a story for the pictures.

c Tell your story to the other group.

How To: **Tell a story**	
Introduction: what is the important news?	_A man and woman were arrested last_
The story: Use sequence words like _then, next, finally._	_Then he tried to_ _Finally, he was_
Conclusion: finish with something funny or a quote.	_The criminal said he didn't remember anything about . . ._

Writing

9 Look at the How To box again and write your story.

Review

1   Complete the sentences with *can('t), could(n't), (will/won't) be able to*, and the verbs in the box. (More than one correct answer may be possible.)

> take   play   stand   sleep   tell   ~~lift~~

Ex: I _can't lift_ this chest. It's too heavy.

1. Alice has an amazing memory. She _____ you the capital city of every country in the world.
2. I didn't take my camera on the trip, so I _____ any photographs.
3. When Michael was younger, he _____ on his hands.
4. I hurt my leg last week, so I _____ tennis tomorrow.
5. I know I look awful. I _____ at all last night.

2   Rewrite the sentences in the passive, starting with the words given.

Ex: Somebody took the keys from my desk.
The keys _were taken from my desk._

1. The police arrested more than 50 people.
    More _____.
2. They opened the doors at exactly 9 A.M.
    The doors _____.
3. They paid me a lot of money to do the job.
    I _____.
4. Nobody met us at the airport.
    We _____.
5. They rescued everybody from the ship.
    Everybody _____.
6. Somebody cleaned all the classrooms yesterday.
    All _____.

3   In three of the sentences below, the word in italics is not correct. Replace the word with a more appropriate one.

>   *receptionist*
Ex: A ~~secretary~~ is usually the first person you meet when you enter a building.

1. She's a very good *interviewee*. She asks just the right questions.

2. I don't have the right *experience* for this job. I don't have a degree in mathematics.

3. They pay us a *salary* 20 percent of our annual salary if we reach our targets.

4. He's decided to *resign*. He wants to spend more time with his family.

Communication | take part in a simple negotiation

4 Look at the suggestions below. Do you agree with them? Can you add any more points?

Five Very Important Tips for Negotiating

1. Negotiating is when two people with different goals work out a solution that is good for both of them. Look at negotiating as a positive process.

2. Before you say what you want, give your reasons. Focus on how your goal will help the other person.

3. Aim high, but always have a back-up plan. For example, if you want a 5% raise, begin by asking for 7%, but be willing to accept 3%.

4. Listen carefully to the other person and let them know you understand their needs. Frequently restate or summarize what they are saying.

5. Never argue or become emotional. A friendly negotiator who tries to find a solution that is good for both people will always come out ahead.

5 ▶2.12 Listen to this "negotiation" and answer these questions.

1. What does each side do "wrong"?
2. What advice would you give each of them to negotiate more successfully?

6a **SPEAKING EXCHANGE** Work in groups of four, two representing Group A and two representing Group B. Practice negotiating. Try to achieve as many of your goals as possible.

Group A: Look at the information on page 127.
Group B: Look at the information on page 129.

b When you have finished negotiating, read the goals of the other group. Who scored the most points?

can, could, be able to for ability

Use *can* or *is/are able to* to say someone has the ability to do something.

> She **can speak** four languages.
>
> **Are** you **able to see** the river?

Use *could* or *was/were able to* to say someone had the ability in the past.

> She **could speak** French by the age of 12.
>
> I **wasn't able to finish** my report.

Use *will be able to* to say someone will have the ability in the future.

> She **won't be able to pass** the test tomorrow.
>
> You**'ll be able to play** golf like a pro soon.

Use expressions like *not at all/not very well/pretty well/very well* to show degrees of ability.

> I can't cook **at all**. ✗✗
>
> He couldn**'t** swim **very well**. ✗
>
> She could sing **pretty well**. ✓
>
> She'll be able to play the guitar **very well** with a few more lessons. ✓✓

Passive voice (past)

Use active verb forms like *gave*, *threw*, and *made* to say what people and things did.

> Sarah **made** a beautiful mirror for Sam's birthday.
>   ↓   ↓
> subject   active verb

Passive verb forms like *was cleaned*, *were taken*, and *was made* are often used to say what happens to things or people or what was done to them.

> This camera **was made** in China.
>   ↓   ↓
> subject   passive verb

The passive is often used when the person or thing that causes the action is unknown or not important.

> This house was built in 1745.

Form: *was/were* + past participle

➕ ➖	I/He/She/It	was wasn't	promoted.
	You/We/They	were weren't	
❓	Was/Wasn't	I/he/she/it	promoted?
	Were/Weren't	you/we/they	
	Yes, No,	I/he/she/it	was. wasn't.
	Yes, No,	you/we/they	were. weren't.

Unit Vocabulary

Jobs

receptionist   secretary   managing director   sales rep

Work

resign	employee	apply for a job
bonus	take a job	be offered a job
salary	education	application form
resumé	experience	work long hours
factory	interviewer	have an interview
company	interviewee	prepare a resumé
employer	get promoted	run your own company

Crime

jury	thief	arrest	punishment
fine	judge	criminal	jail sentence
steal	guilty	innocent	police officer

UNIT 10
Animal planet

Warm Up

1a Look at the photos. Which of the following animals can you see?

eagle	lion	elephant	giraffe	snake	cat	tiger	monkey	bear
horse	cow	flamingo	spider	whale	dog	wolf	dolphin	fish

b **Pair Work** Discuss which animals in the list above are: wild animals, domestic animals, bugs, and sea animals. What other animals do you know in each category?

2a What do you think the expressions below mean?

He eats like a horse.   *There are plenty of fish in the sea.*

b What are some expressions using names of animals in your language?

Reading

1 **Pair Work** Read the article. Then take turns asking and answering the questions below.

Raised by Animals

There are a number of stories about children who were raised by animals. One of the earliest stories is about the twin brothers Romulus and Remus. They were the sons of the god Mars. When they were very young, they were left by the banks of the River Tiber. Luckily, they were found by a wolf. The wolf <u>looked after</u> them and fed them with her milk.

Later, a shepherd <u>came across</u> the boys. He took them home and <u>brought</u> them <u>up</u> as his own children. The boys <u>grew up</u> to be very strong and clever. They decided to build a town in the place where the shepherd found them.

Shortly after building the town, the twins had a big argument. Romulus killed his brother Remus in the fight. Romulus then became the first king of this town, which was named Rome after him.

More recently, two young girls were discovered in the care of a wolf in 1920, in Godamuri, India. The girls (Kamala, 8, and Amala, aged 18 months) were taken to a children's home, but they didn't like their new life there at all. They preferred to be with cats and dogs, and they seemed to <u>look up to</u> animals, not people. They never got along with the other children, and they sometimes bit and attacked them.

The girls slept during the day and were awake at night. They walked on their hands and feet, and enjoyed raw meat. They had extremely good eyesight and hearing. The younger child, Amala, died one year later, but Kamala lived for nine years in the home. She <u>picked up</u> a small number of words, but she remained very different from other children.

1. Who was the father of Romulus and Remus?
2. Where were they left when they were very small?
3. Who found them at first?
4. Who raised them?
5. What did the boys build when they became adults?
6. What happened to Remus?
7. Who first raised Kamala and Amala?
8. How was the girls' relationship with people?
9. What special abilities did they have?
10. What happened to Amala and Kamala?

2 **Group Work** Discuss.

1. Do you think the person who found Kamala and Amala should have left them with the wolf? Why or why not?
2. Do you know of any similar stories in real life or in movies?

Vocabulary | phrasal verbs

3 Match the <u>underlined</u> phrasal verbs from the article with the definitions below.

1. change from child to adult = _____
2. learn without trying = _____
3. take care of = _____
4. raise/educate children = _____
5. find by chance = _____
6. respect = _____

4 **Pair Work** Complete the questions. Then ask and answer them with a partner.

1. Where _____? (you/grow up)
2. Who _____? (bring up/you)
3. As a child, who _____ when you were ill? (look after/you)
4. As a child, who _____? (you/look up to)
5. Have _____ any English from TV or songs? (you/ever/pick up)
6. Have _____ any money in the street? (you/ever/come across)

Pronunciation | sentence stress

5 ▶2.13 **Pair Work** Listen to the sentences in Exercise 4. Mark which words are stressed in each question. Then ask and answer the questions in Exercise 4 with a partner.

Listening and Speaking

6a ▶2.14 Listen to a woman talking about her childhood. Which statement is false?

1. She saw her father occasionally.
2. She grew up in Tokyo.
3. She feels close to her mother and grandmother.
4. She enjoyed school in the United States.

b Listen again and look at the How To box. How many times do you hear each phrase?

How To:	
Use conversational phrases	
Say the same thing in a different way	*I mean, . . .*
Give yourself thinking time before you continue	*Well, . . .*
Go back to your original point	*So, anyway . . .*
Introduce an explanation	*You see, . . .*

7 **Pair Work** Tell another student about your childhood and the people who influenced you most.

Write a short comment on a blog
GRAMMAR nouns: count/noncount

Reading

1 **Pair Work** Read the blog. Then ask and answer the questions below.

WILDLIFE WORLD
BLOG

3 Responses to "Are zoos a good thing?"

Chris, London: Just been to the local zoo with my kids >>> awful! Hated seeing the animals locked up in those tiny cages. So little space. They looked really unhappy, and it seemed quite cruel. :-(

Tania, Boston: Sorry, Chris, that you went to a zoo like that. Most zoos are pretty good, although that one sounds very bad. We have a fantastic zoo here. :-)
The animals have lots of space to move around. I also think it's really important that children can see different animals face-to-face. Then they can learn about them. Also, nearly 12,000 species are in danger of extinction. Zoos can help save some of them!

Gabriela, Acapulco: Although I think Tania's right in some ways, I mainly agree with Chris. Animals shouldn't be locked up. They should be free to go where they want. Yes, it's important that kids have information about animals, but they can get that from the Internet and TV.

Ming, Taipei: Take my advice: take a break and go on a safari in Africa. See the animals in their natural environment. It's completely different from seeing animals in zoos! I don't think I could go to a zoo again.

1. Who is definitely a parent?
2. Who talks about using the Internet for education?
3. Who suggests taking a trip?
4. Who is worried about how much room animals in zoos have?

2 **Group Work** Discuss. Which of the people do you agree or disagree with? Why?

> *Well, I guess I agree with Tania. There are some very nice zoos, and the animals are taken care of well.*

> *Really? Which zoos are you thinking of?*

Grammar | nouns: count/noncount

3a Look at the sentences. Which <u>underlined</u> noun is count and which is noncount?

   1. The <u>animals</u> have lots of space.   2. It's important that kids have <u>information</u> about animals.

b Put the following nouns into the correct columns in the Active Grammar box.

> vacation   newspaper   news   tourism   job   money
> furniture   ~~information~~   work   advice   bill   ~~animal~~

Active Grammar

Count	Noncount
animal,	_information,_
1. Can be singular or plural.	1. Do not use *a* or *an*.
2. Use *a few*, *some*, or *a lot of* in positive sentences.	2. Use *a little*, *a little bit of*, *a piece of*, *some*, or *a lot of* in positive sentences.
3. Use *any* or *many* in negative and questions.	3. Use *any* or *much* in negatives and questions.

See Reference page 106

4 Choose the correct alternatives.

   1. This job will involve *many/a lot of* hard work.

   2. We don't have *a little/much* furniture.

   3. I've got *any/some* bad news. It's going to rain.

   4. I have *a few/a little* bills that I need to pay.

   5. I need *a little/a few* advice.

   6. I'd like to move, but I don't have *many/much* money.

Writing

5 Read the blog in the Writing bank on page 136. Do the exercises.

6a **Pair Work** Choose one of the topics below and start an "online" blog discussion (on paper). In pairs, write your opinions about this topic.

   1. Are there good reasons for keeping animals in zoos?

   2. Is it wrong to wear fur or leather?

   3. Is it necessary to use animals for scientific research?

b **Group Work** Exchange papers with another pair of students to continue the discussion.

Speculate about sounds and pictures

GRAMMAR articles: *the*

Listening

1 ▶2.15 Listen to a news report about a dog-friendly hotel and complete the information below.

Inn by the Sea has welcomed dogs for over
_____ (1.). It offers all dog guests a free water bowl,
beach _____, (2.) blankets, and treats. Owners get a list
of nearby _____, (3.) dog-friendly beaches, and parks.

The **Inn-credible Pet** package is the perfect getaway for you
and your dog. It includes:

- two nights in a _____ (4.)
- a welcome _____ (5.) and a personalized _____ (6.)
- dinner from the gourmet _____ (7.) (includes "the bird dog" with grilled _____ (8.) or "doggy gumbo" with Angus _____ (9.))
- locally made _____ (10.) at bedtime
- 30-minute in-room _____ (11.)

The **Inn-credible Pet** package starts at $_____ (12.)/night.

2 **Pair Work** Discuss.

What do you think of the Inn-credible Pet package?

Vocabulary | verbs + prepositions

3a Add the correct preposition from the box to the questions below. You will use some words more than once.

> about   in   of   on   to   with

1. When you meet a dog, do you ever worry _____ being bitten? Explain.
2. Does the idea of staying at a dog-friendly resort appeal _____ you? Why or why not?
3. Have you ever heard _____ any dog-friendly hotels in your country? Explain.
4. Many pet owners think all parks should allow dogs to be off the leash. Do you agree _____ them? Why or why not?
5. Did you ever dream _____ having a pet when you were a kid? What kind of animal did you want?
6. Have you ever spent money _____ a present for a pet? If yes, how much did you spend on it?
7. Do you believe _____ treating dogs and cats like people? Explain.
8. What do you think about people who share the food on their plate _____ their pet?

b **Pair Work** Discuss the questions above with a partner. Use the verb and preposition in your answer.

Grammar | articles: *the*

4 Match the sentences below to the rules in the Active Grammar box.

    a. Inn by the Sea has welcomed dogs for over 15 years.

    b. It is designed to appeal to the pickiest eater.

    c. The Inn offers a special package. The package includes two nights.

Active Grammar

_____ **1.** Use *the* with superlatives because there is only one.
    *He's **the youngest** person in the company.*

_____ **2.** Use *the* to refer to something or someone you have mentioned before.
    *She has **a cat** and a dog. **The cat** is nearly 12.*

_____ **3.** Don't use *the* to talk about things or people in general.
    ***Children** can be very funny.*

See Reference page 106

5a Four of the sentences have mistakes. Find and correct them.

          the
    Ex: What's ‸ most interesting thing you've done recently?

    1. Do you prefer the cats or dogs? Why?

    2. Who's the funniest person you know?

    3. How long have you known your best friend?

    4. At what age do you think the children should be allowed to drop out of school?

    5. Did you like the school(s) that you went to?

    6. What's most beautiful place you have been to?

    7. Do you think that the money makes you happy?

    8. Is public transportation expensive in your country?

b **Pair Work** Ask and answer the questions above.

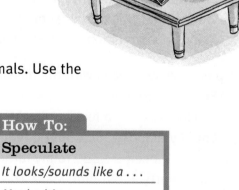

She's the most intelligent pet I've ever had!

Speaking

6a ▶2.16 **Pair Work** Listen to six sounds made by animals. Use the How To box to say what you think each sound is.

b **SPEAKING EXCHANGE** Now look at the pictures on page 132. What animals do you think these pictures might show?

What do you think this first picture shows?

Hmm . . . It could be a . . .

How To:
Speculate

It looks/sounds like a . . .

Maybe it's a . . .

It could be a . . .

Review

1 Complete the sentences with *a/an*, *the*, or nothing (Ø).

   Ex: What's __the__ longest river in South America?

   1. I had _____ sandwich and _____ banana for lunch, but _____ sandwich was awful!
   2. Simon is looking for _____ job in publishing.
   3. Did you pass _____ test you took last month?
   4. Listening to _____ music helps me relax.
   5. Yesterday was _____ hottest day of the year.
   6. Where is the main entrance to _____ building?

2 Read the sentences. Circle the correct choice.

   Ex: I only speak *a little*/*a few* words of French.

   1. We don't have *much*/*many* rain in the summer.
   2. She has *a lot*/*some* of experience.
   3. He gave me a good *piece*/*lot* of advice.
   4. I need *some*/*little* paper to write on.
   5. Could I have *a little*/*few* more cake?
   6. Do *many*/*much* tourists come here?
   7. I don't have *a lot of*/*many* time today.

3 Complete the sentences with prepositions from the box. You will use some words more than once.

in	on	to	with	about	of

   Ex: I've heard __of__ that organization.

   1. He always dreamed _____ having a big aquarium.
   2. I don't believe _____ wearing fur or leather.
   3. I think we should get a cat, but Tim doesn't agree _____ me.
   4. It's amazing how much we spend _____ dog food each week!
   5. Have you ever heard _____ a white flamingo?
   6. She worries _____ her horse. He's been a little sick.
   7. We feel that this ad will appeal _____ cat and dog owners.
   8. Many lions don't like to share their food _____ each other.

4 Complete the sentences with the missing words.

   Ex: He's eating like a __horse__. He must be hungry.

   1. I picked _____ a few words of Spanish on my vacation.
   2. Could you look _____ our dog for a few days while we're away?
   3. I really looked _____ to my father when I was a child.
   4. Don't worry about him, Mary. There are plenty of _____ in the sea!
   5. She was as quiet as a _____ when she was a child. She hardly ever said a word!
   6. I don't think Sunita's parents brought her _____ very well. She behaves very badly.

Communication | participate in making a group decision

5 Read the information about the animal protection organizations and answer the questions.
Which organization:

1. works all around the world on a number of issues?
2. offers you the chance to feed an animal?
3. has animal inspectors?

WWF the global conservation organization

WWF works on both global and local environmental issues.

- We protect animals in danger, such as tigers and whales.
- We protect areas in danger, such as forests and seas.
- We protect the planet from dangers, such as climate change and toxic chemicals.

Make a donation by credit or debit card

Help support our conservation work by making a donation to WWF today.

For more information go to: www.wwf.org

6a **Group Work** Your class has recently won $3,000. You can give this money to one or more of these charities. Or you can spend it to help animals in another way. In groups of four, brainstorm ways of spending the money. Then decide how you want to spend the $3,000.

b Explain your decisions to other students. Listen to the ideas from the other groups. Are they similar to or different from your group's decision?

> *My group decided to donate $1,000 to . . .*

Elephants are majestic creatures that are highly intelligent, complex, social, and sensitive individuals. The Elephant Sanctuary in Tennessee is the largest natural habitat refuge in the US developed specifically for endangered Asian and African elephants. The Sanctuary is designed for old, sick, or needy elephants who have been retired from zoos and circuses. Our residents are not required to perform or entertain for the public; instead, they are encouraged to live like elephants.

the Elephant Sanctuary® in Tennessee

How You Can Help

It costs $125,000 annually to provide sanctuary for one elephant. Here's how you can help. For $30 you can feed one of our 15 elephants for one day. For $60 you can feed two of them, and for $540 you can feed them all for a day.

 The RSPCA (Royal Society for the Prevention of Cruelty to Animals)

Action for animals

RSPCA inspectors in the UK work around the clock to save animals in distress. Last year, inspectors investigated over 100,000 complaints of cruelty to animals.

Preventing cruelty

Our inspectors prefer to educate people rather than prosecute. They also offer help and advice about the care of animals in markets, pet shops, kennels, and farms.

Our inspectors help animals in distress—last year they removed over 180,000 animals from danger or abuse and rescued over 11,000 injured or trapped animals.

Get involved

Your support can make the difference between life and death to an injured, sick, or neglected animal.

Unit 10 Reference

Count/Noncount nouns

Count nouns are words like *animal*, *child*, *zoo*. They can be singular or plural.

Noncount nouns are words like *information*, *advice*, *news*.

Here are other examples of noncount nouns.

behavior	bread	salt
furniture	health	work
research	trouble	traffic
knowledge	luggage	travel
spaghetti	weather	water

The following nouns can be count or noncount.

chicken	glass	hair	iron	paper
room	space	time	wine	soda

Compare: *Would you like a soda?* and *I drink too much soda.*

Use *a/an, a few, some, any, many, a lot of* before count nouns.

> There weren't **many people** at the party.
> They've got **a lot of friends** in Australia.
> You should rest for **a few days**.

Use *a little/a little bit of* (and sometimes *a piece of*), *some, any, much, a lot of* before noncount nouns.

> How **much salt** did you put in this?
> We bought **a lot of bread** this morning.
> Can you give me **a piece of advice**?

Some is most common in affirmative clauses; *any* is common in questions and negatives.

> I'd like **some information**.
> Have you been to **any** interesting **places**?
> I didn't bring **any money** with me.

Use *some* in questions if the answer is expected to be *Yes*.

> Could I have **some dessert**, please?

Use *many* with count nouns and *much* with noncount nouns.

> I don't have **much time**.
> Did you bring **many CDs**?

The definite article

Superlatives use *the*, because they refer to only one, and it is usually clear which one.

> She's **the best player** in the team.

Use *the* when referring to something or someone we mentioned before.

> I bought some ham and **some chicken**. We had **the chicken** for lunch.

Use *the* in a number of expressions referring to the physical environment.

> Would you like to live in **the country**?
> Listen to **the rain**!
> What do you think **the weather** will be like this weekend?

In most cases, do not use *the* to talk about things or people in **general**. Use *the* to talk about **particular** people or things.

> People watch too much **TV** these days.
> There's a problem with **the TV**. There's a picture but no sound.

Unit Vocabulary

Animals

monkey	dog	tiger	horse
giraffe	cat	bear	snake
dolphin	cow	lion	spider
flamingo	wolf	eagle	whale
elephant	fish		

Animal idioms

eat like a horse	plenty of fish in the sea
as quiet as a mouse	

Phrasal verbs

grow up	bring up	come across
pick up	look up to	look after

Verb + preposition

appeal to	spend on	worry about
listen to	agree with	dream of
hear of	share with	believe in

UNIT 11
World travel

Warm Up

1 **Pair Work** Discuss.

1. Where do you think each photograph was taken? Why?
2. What forms of transportation do you see?
3. What verbs do you associate with each of these forms of transportation?

2 **Pair Work** Fill in the blanks with the correct verb from the box. Then ask and answer with a partner.

ride	missed	gotten off
drive	took	taken

1. Do you usually _____ your car to work?
2. Do you ever _____ your bicycle to work?
3. When was the last time you _____ a taxi?
4. Have you ever _____ a train at the wrong station?
5. Have you ever _____ an overnight trip on a train or bus?
6. Have you ever arrived at the airport late and _____ your flight?

Find out if someone would be a good travel companion

CAN DO ✓

GRAMMAR present perfect with *just*, *yet*, and *already*

Reading

1   **Pair Work** Read the excerpt from Lucy's travel diary.
    Then discuss what annoys her.

> **Saturday**
> I can't believe it! I'm in Rio, 4,000 miles from home, and I've just bumped into Andy, from my old school. We're going to travel to Salvador together. It's great to see him again!
>
> **Sunday**
> On the bus—10:15 A.M. Bad news. Andy has already started to annoy me. He won't stop talking! Oh well . . . I'm sure it'll get better.   3:30 P.M. I can't stand it! He hasn't stopped talking yet. I now know everything about his friends, his family, even his neighbor's cat!   4:30 P.M. Andy's just fallen asleep, but now he's started snoring! Arrgh!
>
> **Monday**
> On the beach—12:30 P.M. I'm exhausted—I didn't get any sleep because of HIM. And I've just spent the whole morning listening to Andy complaining about the weather, the food, even the beach! What am I going to do?
>
> **Tuesday**
> In a café—2:30 P.M. Now he's started singing to himself. I have to tell him I can't travel with him any more. He's driving me crazy . . .

2a **Pair Work** Roleplay a conversation in which Lucy tells Andy that she
    doesn't want to travel with him any more.

b   ▶ 2.17 Listen and compare your conversation with the recorded one.
    Discuss what is the same and what is different.

Grammar | present perfect with *just*, *yet*, and *already*

3   Look at the Active Grammar box and complete
    the rules with *just*, *yet*, or *already*.

4   Write *just*, *already*, or *yet* in the correct place
    in each sentence.
    Ex: I've ^*just* had lunch. (I had lunch five
        minutes ago.)
    1. Pedro's left the party. (It's only 9:00.)
    2. Noriko hasn't called. (I expected her to
       call earlier.)
    3. I've spent all my money. (I didn't expect
       to spend it all so early.)
    4. My parents have come back from Miami.
       (They came back two hours ago.)

> **Active Grammar**
>
> We often use *just*, *yet*, and *already* with the
> present perfect.
>
> *Andy has **already** started to annoy me.*
>
> *He hasn't stopped talking **yet**.*
>
> *He's **just** fallen asleep.*
>
> 1. _____ means a very short time ago.
>
> 2. _____ shows that something
>   happened sooner than expected.
>
> 3. _____ shows that the speaker
>   expected something to happen before now.

See Reference page 116

5   **SPEAKING EXCHANGE** Look at the picture on page 132. With a partner, take turns
    saying what Lucy's *just done*, *has already done*, and what she *hasn't done yet*.

> *Lucy has just taken a shower.*

Vocabulary | vacation activities

6a Match the photos (A–D) with the types of activities.

> _____ go sightseeing _____ hang out at the beach
>
> _____ go camping _____ go skiing/snowboarding

b Match the opposite pairs.

A	B
_b_ 1. rent a car	a. get a last-minute deal
_____ 2. go abroad	b. use local transportation
_____ 3. stay in hotels	c. go to bed early
_____ 4. book early	d. travel in your own country
_____ 5. go out	e. rent an apartment

7 **Pair Work** Tell your partner about a nice vacation you had. Use the How To box to help you.

How To:

Talk about a vacation you've had

When . . . ?	_I went on vacation last July._
What . . . ? Where . . . ? How long . . . ?	_It was a two-week trip to Tahiti._
Booking	_We got a last-minute deal._
Accommodations	_We stayed in a great hotel._
Activity	_We went swimming every day._

Speaking and Writing

8a ▶2.18 You're going to find a travel companion. Listen and write down the questions you hear.

1. _____ 4. _____
2. _____ 5. _____
3. _____ 6. _____

b Write two more questions to ask.

7. _____ 8. _____

9a **Group Work** Ask and answer the questions with other students.

b Decide who the best travel companion is for you. Write a paragraph explaining why.

> I think Maria is the best travel companion for me. She
> likes to do a lot of the same things I do. She . . .

Make generalizations about customs CAN DO

GRAMMAR verbs with direct and indirect objects

A B C D E

Vocabulary | greetings and leave taking

1a Match the words and phrases with the photos above.

> _____ wave _____ kiss
>
> _____ bow _____ give a gift
>
> _____ shake hands (with)

b Complete the sentences using the correct form of the verbs in the box.

> **Ex:** In Japan, you should _give a gift_ using both hands.

1. In most countries, people _____ when they say goodbye.

2. In most Western countries, people usually _____ when they meet in a business situation.

3. In Asia, people usually _____ when they meet in a business situation.

4. In the US, men don't _____ on the cheeks when they meet in a business situation.

Reading

2a **SPEAKING EXCHANGE** Work in two groups.

Group A: Read the article on the right.

Group B: Read the article on page 130.

ADVICE FOR BUSINESS TRAVELERS

GIVING GIFTS

Japan

Gift-giving is very important in Japan, and it usually happens at the end of a visit. A souvenir from your country is a good idea. If you give flowers, avoid giving four or nine flowers, as these are unlucky numbers.

China

Chinese people will probably refuse your gift several times, but it is polite to continue offering it to them. Do not give clocks in China, as the Chinese phrase "give a clock" is similar to the phrase "say goodbye (to the dead)."

Middle East

Give gifts of the highest quality leather, silver, or crystal. Remember to avoid alcohol and leather made from pigs.

South America

Gift-giving is less formal in South America but still an important part of the culture. Avoid leather, as many of the world's best leather products come from South America.

Australia, Canada, US, and Europe

Gift-giving in these countries is informal and not always expected. However, it is polite to bring someone flowers or wine when visiting their house. In some European countries, you should avoid red flowers (associated with romance).

b **Pair Work** Work with a student from the other group. Student A: ask these questions. Then answer Student B's questions.

1. Should you use first names in Germany?
2. In which part of the world do people stand closest to each other?
3. Why don't people from the US like you to stand too close to them?
4. Should you show how strong you are when you shake hands?
5. Do Asians ever shake hands?
6. Do business people kiss each other in Russia?

3 **Pair Work** Read the saying below and discuss the questions.

"When in Rome, do as the Romans do."

1. What does the saying mean?
2. Do you agree with it? Why or why not?

Grammar | verbs with direct and indirect objects

4 Read the Active Grammar box. Write *to* or Ø (nothing) in sentences 3a and b at the bottom of the box.

5 **Pair Work** Take turns rearranging the words to correct the sentences.

Ex: Our company more choices offers you.

> Our company offers you more choices.

1. I lent to him $20 about three weeks ago.
2. Could you bring that book me when you come?
3. He sent to her a huge bunch of flowers.
4. Would you like to tell anything me?
5. We should a special gift give our hosts.

Active Grammar

1. Some verbs can be followed by a direct object and an indirect object:

   *He gave **his boss** **a present**.*

   indirect object · direct object

2. The indirect object is usually a person and comes first. Two forms are possible.

   a. verb + indirect object + direct object
   b. verb + direct object + *to* + indirect object

   Form (*a*) is more natural, especially when the indirect object is a pronoun (*me, him, them*, etc.).

3. Common verbs that take two objects are: *give, bring, offer, lend, owe, send, tell, promise.*

   a. *It is polite to bring _____ your host flowers.*
   b. *It is polite to bring flowers _____ your host.*

See Reference page 116

Speaking

6 **Pair Work** Tell your partner about customs in your country (or a country you know well). Use the language in the How To box to help you.

How To:

Make generalizations about groups of people	
Use nationalities/ adjectives + *people*	*Chinese people, Young people, Rich people, . . .*
Make generalizations	*. . . **tend** to talk about the weather.* *. . . don't **generally**/**usually** give gifts.*

Ideas
giving gifts · birthdays
visiting someone's house
an important national festival

> Young people don't usually give gifts on . . .

Write about a place you've traveled to

GRAMMAR past perfect

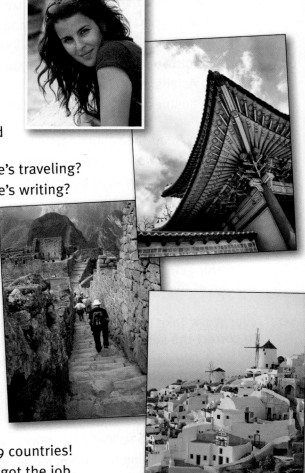

Listening

1 ▶2.19 Listen to the first part of an interview with a travel writer and answer these questions.

1. How did she start traveling?
2. How did she start writing?
3. What was her first "break" as a travel writer?

2a ▶2.20 Listen to the second part of the interview and answer these questions.

1. What is the most difficult thing for her when she's traveling?
2. What is the most difficult thing for her when she's writing?
3. Which travel writer influenced her the most?
4. What advice does she give to someone thinking of being a travel writer?

3 **Pair Work** Discuss.

1. Do you agree that being a travel writer is a "dream job"? Why or why not?
2. Which country would you most like to travel to and write about? Why?

Grammar | past perfect

4a ▶2.21 Listen and complete the sentences.

1. By the time I was 16, I _____ 19 countries!
2. I _____ there very long when I got the job.
3. _____ any other books before this one was published?

b Look at the Active Grammar box. Write *before* or *after* to complete the rule.

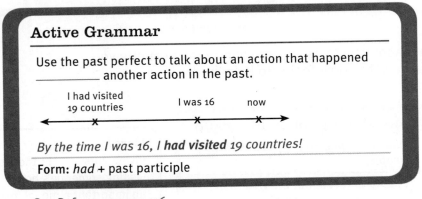

> ### Active Grammar
>
> Use the past perfect to talk about an action that happened _____ another action in the past.
>
> | I had visited 19 countries | I was 16 | now |
>
> ←——×————————×————————×——→
>
> *By the time I was 16, I **had visited** 19 countries!*
>
> **Form:** *had* + past participle

See Reference page 116

5 Circle the best choice to complete each sentence.

1. We got to the theater late. The play *began/had begun*.
2. I saw a car by the side of the road. It *ran/had run* out of gas.
3. I phoned Jack, but he wasn't there. He *went/had gone* out.
4. Sorry I'm late. The car *had/had had* a flat tire on the way.
5. It was my first time in Egypt. I *didn't go/hadn't been* there before.

6 Put one verb in parentheses in the past perfect and one verb in the simple past in each sentence.

1. By the time I _____ (arrive) at the station, the train _____ (leave).
2. When we _____ (get) there, we realized we _____ (not/pack) enough warm clothes.
3. I _____ (decide) to go back to the same place I _____ (go) on my last vacation.
4. As soon as I saw Carolina, I _____ (realize) I _____ (meet) her before.

Pronunciation | past perfect contractions

7 ▶2.22 Listen to sentences 1–4 from Exercise 6. How do you pronounce *had* in the past perfect in each one? Repeat the sentences with natural pronunciation.

Speaking and Writing

8 **Pair Work** Read the paragraph about Havana. Then work with a partner to find examples of:

1. adjectives: senses (taste, smell, etc.) and colors. What do they describe?
2. the past perfect. Why is it used?

Last summer we went to Havana, the capital of Cuba. It's a really interesting city—full of old cars, bicycles, friendly people, and of course music. The weather was hot, even in the evenings, and music came from every bar. The sound of trumpets and drums was everywhere.

One evening we stopped in a bar with a yellow door. It looked like many of the old buildings in Havana—unpainted for years. But the food and the coffee were fantastic. I had never tasted such delicious coffee before.

9 You're going to do some travel writing. Follow these instructions.

1. Think of a place you have traveled to (a beach, a town, etc.) and make notes about the place.
2. **Pair Work** Tell your partner about your place and ask questions about your partner's place.
3. Write about your place. (Use about 100 words.)

Review

1 Circle the correct word to complete each conversation.

> **Ex: A:** Where are you going on your vacation?
>
> **B:** I've haven't decided (yet)/already.

1. **A:** Do you want to see that movie?
   B: No, I've seen it _yet/already_.

2. **A:** Have you booked the tickets _just/yet_?
   B: No, I'll do it today.

3. **A:** Why is your hair wet?
   B: I've _just/already_ taken a shower.

4. **A:** Have you cleaned the kitchen?
   B: No, I haven't done it _already/yet_.

5. **A:** Would you like some lunch?
   B: No, thanks. I've _yet/just_ had some.

6. **A:** I'd like to buy Mei that new CD.
   B: She's _yet/already_ bought it.

2 Put the words in the correct order.

> **Ex:** anyone/You/money/shouldn't/to/lend   _You shouldn't lend money to anyone._

1. owes/a lot of money/me/Juan _____

2. I/Can/some tea/you/offer? _____

3. a raise/He/this month/me/promised _____

4. always/me/My grandmother/good advice/gives _____

5. my mother/I/some flowers/sent/to _____

6. the bill/us/Could/bring/please/you? _____

3 Put one verb in parentheses in the simple past and one verb in the past perfect in each sentence.

> **Ex:** I _wanted_ (want) to read something, but I _hadn't brought_ (not/bring) my book.

1. She _____ (want) to buy a purse she _____ (see) the day before.

2. When I _____ (arrive) at the airport, I realized I _____ (miss) my plane.

3. As soon as I _____ (close) the door, I remembered I _____ (leave) my keys inside.

4. After I _____ (eat) breakfast, I _____ (feel) better.

5. When I _____ (see) the exam, I realized I _____ (not/study) enough.

6. When she _____ (try) to pay for it, she realized she _____ (forgot) her credit card.

4 Complete the sentences, using the correct form of the verbs in the box.

> have   get   shake   rent   wave   ~~unpack~~

> **Ex:** When I arrived at the hotel, I _unpacked_ and put all my clothes in the closet.

1. Should I _____ hands with the boss when I meet her?

2. Go on the Internet and see if you can _____ a last-minute deal.

3. Sorry I'm late. I _____ a flat tire on the way.

4. When I was on Maui, I _____ a car to see the island.

5. The train left the station and we all _____ goodbye to them.

Communication | get information necessary for travel

5   **Group Work** Discuss.

1. Have you ever bought a train, bus, or plane ticket in another country? If yes, explain.
2. What was the last time you took a trip on a train or bus? Where did you go? How was it?

6a   ▶ **2.23** Listen to a customer and clerk at a ticket booth in New York's Grand Central Station. Fill in the blanks in the conversation below.

A: Hi. Can I help you?

B: Yes, I'd like _____ (1.) to Scarsdale, please.

A: One-way or round-trip?

B: _____ (2.), please.

A: That'll be $16.

B: Can I pay by _____ (3.)?

A: Yes, just swipe your card there and _____ (4.) PIN.

B: Oh, OK. And when is the next train?

A: The next train is at 8:24.

B: _____ (5.) will it be on?

A: It'll be on track 21.

B: Twenty-one. And what time does it _____ (6.) Scarsdale?

A: It arrives in Scarsdale at . . . 9:06.

B: Great, thanks.

A: Here's your ticket. Have a _____ (7.).

American English	British English
one-way or round-trip?	single or return?

b   Listen again and repeat the conversation.

7a   **Pair Work** Practice the conversation with a partner. Change roles and practice again. Then practice the conversation without looking at the page.

b   **SPEAKING EXCHANGE** Work with a partner.

     Student A: Follow the directions on page 129.
     Student B: Follow the directions on page 130.

Unit 11 Reference

Present perfect with *just, yet,* and *already*

Form the present perfect with *has/have* + past participle.

Use *just, yet,* and *already* with the present perfect.

Just means a "short time ago." *Just* usually comes between *has/have* and the past participle.

> **I've just seen** a really great movie.
>
> **Have** you **just arrived**?

Already shows that something happened sooner than the speaker expected. *Already* usually comes between *has/have* and the past participle or at the end of the sentence.

> You**'ve already told** me that.
>
> He**'s taken** his driving test six times **already**.

Yet means "until now" and shows that the speaker is expecting something to happen. *Yet* usually comes at the end of questions and negative sentences.

> **Have** you **seen** Dave **yet**?
>
> I **haven't gotten** the tickets **yet**.

Verbs with direct and indirect objects

Some verbs can be followed by both a direct object and an indirect object. The indirect object usually refers to a person and comes first:

verb + indirect object + direct object

> He gave <u>**his wife**</u> <u>some earrings</u> for her birthday.

The indirect object can also come after the direct object. In this case, use *to* before the indirect object:

verb + direct object + *to* + indirect object

> He gave <u>some earrings</u> <u>**to his wife**</u> for her birthday.

However, it is more natural to use: verb + indirect object + direct object, especially when the indirect object is a pronoun (*me, you, him, her, it, us, them*).

> He gave **her** some earrings for her birthday.

Some verbs commonly followed by two objects are:

give, bring, offer, lend, owe, send, tell, promise, buy, teach, show, write

Past perfect

Use the past perfect to talk about an action or actions that happened before another action in the past.

> When I saw him, I realized **I'd met** him before.

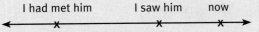

I had met him   I saw him   now

Form the past perfect with *had* + past participle.

> I ate like a horse because I **hadn't eaten** all day.

The past perfect is common after verbs of "saying" or "thinking":

> **I told her** we had bought the tickets.
>
> **She realized** she'd met him before somewhere.

Unit Vocabulary

Transportation

bicycle   bus   car   plane   taxi   train

Verb phrases about travel

get on or off a bus/train/plane/bicycle
take a bus/train/plane/taxi
miss a bus/train/plane
ride a bicycle

go sightseeing	hang out at the beach
go camping	go skiing/snowboarding
rent a car	use local transportation
go abroad	travel in your own country
stay in hotels	get a last-minute deal
book early	

Greetings and presents

shake hands (with someone)	a handshake
bow (to someone)	kiss (someone)
a kiss wave (to someone)	a wave
give a present or gift	a bow

UNIT 12
Money matters

A

B

C

D

Warm Up

1   **Pair Work** What is happening in each of the photos? Discuss.

2   Complete each question with words from the box. Then in pairs answer the questions.

> earn   withdraw   spending   borrowing   lending   save

American English	British English
ATM	cashpoint

1. How do you feel about _____ money to friends?
2. How do you feel about _____ money from your friends or family?
3. How often do you _____ cash from an ATM?
4. Do you try to _____ any money each month? If so, is it difficult?
5. What do you enjoy _____ money on? Do you usually shop online or in person?
6. How much do nurses, teachers, and lawyers typically _____ each year in your country? Do you think this is right?

Say what you'd do in a hypothetical situation

Reading

1 **Pair Work** Read the article. Then take turns asking and answering the questions below.

Q: Do most people cheat?
A: Yes, but just a little.

If your teacher gave you the answer key to a test and asked you to grade yourself, would you cheat? How about if your teacher gave you money for every correct answer? The magazine *SmartMoney* recently reported a study by professors Mazar and Ariely that looked into just that question. The study involved 791 students. The students were given an answer key and told to grade themselves on a simple test, with a financial reward for each right answer. The researchers wanted to know how many students would cheat.

   The bad news is that the researchers found most students cheated. But the good news is that most students cheated only a little—on about 7–17 percent of the test items. And very few students cheated on all the test items—just 5 students out of the 791. One very interesting finding was the effect of money. If students got $2.50 or $10.00 for each correct answer, they cheated less. If students got just 10 or 50 cents for each answer, they cheated more.

1. What were students asked to do in the study?
2. Were most students honest when grading themselves?
3. How much did most students cheat?
4. How did the amount of money they got for each test item affect how much they cheated?

2 **Group Work** Discuss. Why do you think students cheated more if they got less money for each answer?

Vocabulary | money

3 Match the phrases in A to the phrases in B.

A	B
1. pay for something _d_	a. on money that you borrow
2. pay <u>interest</u> ____	b. when you retire
3. get a <u>pension</u> ____	c. for working a 40-hour week
4. earn a <u>salary</u> ____	d. with <u>cash</u>
5. pay <u>taxes</u> ____	e. to the government

4a Complete the sentences using the <u>underlined</u> words from Exercise 3.
1. Do you usually pay for things with _____, with a debit card, or with a credit card?
2. How much _____ do you pay when you borrow money from a bank?
3. Do you think the _____ you pay to the government are too high?
4. Does your company offer a _____ plan for retirement?
5. What is an average _____ in your country?

b **Pair Work** Discuss the questions above.

Grammar | unreal conditional

5 Read the examples in the Active Grammar box. Circle the correct choices to complete the rules.

> ### Active Grammar
>
> **The unreal conditional refers to imaginary situations.**
> *If a cashier gave me too much money back, I would tell him or her.*
> *I would go on a cruise if I won the lottery.*
>
> 1. The unreal conditional refers to <u>past</u> / <u>present and future</u> time.
>
> 2. The *if* clause comes <u>first</u> / <u>first or second</u>.
>
> **Form:** *If* + simple past, *would* + verb

See Reference page 126

6 Put the words in the correct order.

1. had/you/If you/would/a dog/exercise/get/more

   _____

2. he/his exams/pass/worked/He/if/would/harder

   _____

3. She/if/much/her boyfriend/be/would/she left/happier

   _____

4. spoke/job/easier/German/I/much/my/be/If/would

   _____

5. If/a car/I/to/had/would/to work/I/drive

   _____
   _____

Speaking

7a Look at the picture. What would you do if you saw this happening?

> *If I saw someone trying to steal CDs in a store, I would . . .*

b **Pair Work** Read each situation. Discuss what you would do.

1. A store clerk gives you back an extra $10 by mistake.

2. You find a wallet in the street. There is no ID in it, but there is $200 in cash.

3. A builder is doing some work on your house. He asks you to pay in cash so that he doesn't have to pay any taxes.

4. A friend has just bought a very expensive new jacket. You think it looks awful. She asks you your opinion.

5. A friend doesn't have much money. He suggests you go out to a restaurant together and then leave before the waiter brings the bill.

Report what someone said to you

GRAMMAR reported speech

Listening

1 **Pair Work** Discuss.

1. Were you a good student in school? Why or why not?
2. Who was your favorite teacher? What was your favorite subject? Why?

2a ▶2.24 Listen to the news segment and answer the questions.

1. What has Hamilton High School done?
2. How do people feel about the program?

b **Group Work** What is your opinion of this program? Discuss.

Grammar | reported speech

3 ▶2.25 Listen to the end of the news segment again. Read the rules and complete examples a–c from the news segment in the Active Grammar box below.

Active Grammar _____

1. To report what someone said, use *say* or *tell*.
   *He **said (that)** it was a good idea.*   *He **told me (that)** it was a good idea.*

2. Change the tense in the reported statement:
   present → past   past/present perfect → past perfect   <u>will</u>/<u>can</u> → <u>would</u>/<u>could</u>
   Change the pronoun if necessary.
   "He's our teacher."   *She said that he **was their** teacher.*

   a. "More students have gotten into college this year than ever before."
      (He) told me that more students _____ into college this year.

   b. "I think it's a great idea."
      She said that she _____ it _____ a great idea.

   c. "I'm going to buy a new computer."
      She said she _____ a new computer.

See Reference page 126

4 Anna is talking to Pete. Change her direct speech to reported speech. Begin with the words given.

1. "I prefer studying in the evening." Anna said _____
2. "I'm working at a local college." Anna told _____
3. "Mark saw Terry in the bookstore." Anna said _____
4. "They haven't lived here for long." Anna told _____
5. "My notes were on the table." Anna said _____
6. "I'll speak to my economics professor." Anna said _____

Speaking

5 **Group Work** Ask different classmates each question and complete the chart. When you answer another student's questions, refer to the How To box below and explain your answers.

Question	Name	Answer
1 Do you think it's a good idea to pay students to do well on tests?		
2 Do you think tests are necessary?		
3 Do you usually do well or poorly on tests?		
4 Do you think children under ten should have to take tests?		

How To:

Deal with difficult questions	
If you don't want to answer	**A:** *Were you a straight-A student?* **B:** *I'm not telling!*
If you didn't understand the question	**A:** *Could you give me a hand?* **B:** *Sorry, what do you mean?* **A:** *Could you help me?*
If you need time to think of an answer	**A:** *That's a good question. Let me think . . .*

6 **Pair Work** Show your chart to another student. Explain why each person gave their answers.

> *Lian thinks it's a good idea to pay students to do well on tests. She said that it would help them to work harder.*

Writing

7a Look at the formal letter on page 134 in the Writing bank. Do the exercises.

b Look at the ad below. Write a formal letter to Hilltop University to ask for more information.

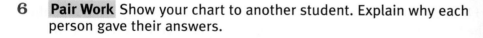

HILLTOP UNIVERSITY

Hilltop University is located in beautiful Colorado.
We now offer some students money to take some of our courses.
Study and earn at the same time!

For more information, please write to:
The Admissions Department
Hilltop University
Limon, Colorado 80828

Possible questions
What classes are offered?
How much money can students get?
What are admissions requirements?

Reading

1 **Pair Work** Discuss.

1. What is the game in the photo?
2. What is the goal of the game?
3. Why do you think a baseball might be worth $1 million?

2 Read the article. Then answer the questions below.

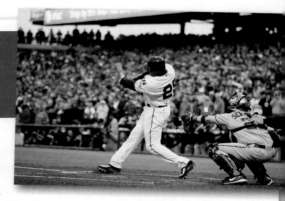

The strange story of the $1 million baseball

San Francisco Giants player Barry Bonds hit a record-breaking home run in 2001. It was his 73rd home run of the season, and many fans knew the ball would be worth a lot of money—close to $1 million. Two men, Alex Popov and
5 Patrick Hayashi, were both in the area where the ball flew. And both men were wearing baseball gloves in the hope of catching the ball. When the ball went into the stands, it hit Popov's glove. Surrounding fans pushed and grabbed for the ball, and it was Hayashi who ended up with it. He held it in the air, and baseball officials gave him a certificate saying it was his.

Popov decided to take Hayashi to court. Many fans argued that the two men should just sell the ball
10 and split the million, but Popov was determined the ball was his. A little over a year later, the men had their time in court. The judge considered the case for four months. He didn't agree with either man that the ball was his alone. He said the ball belonged to neither of them and that they should sell the ball and split the money. The ball was finally sold at auction a few months later. Unfortunately for the men, a home-run baseball is worth the most just after it has been hit. The ball sold for $450,000,
15 leaving each man $225,000. But Mr. Popov's lawyer sued him, saying Popov owed him $473,500 in legal fees.

1. Why was the ball worth $1 million?
2. Why did Popov lose the ball?
3. What did Hayashi get from the officials?
4. What did Popov do after the game?
5. What did the judge decide? Why?
6. What do you think Popov did with his money?

Vocabulary | context clues

3 **Pair Work** Find the following words in the article. Look at the context. Discuss what you think the words might mean.

1. the stands (line 6)
2. grabbed (line 7)
3. ended up (line 7)
4. officials (line 8)
5. take to court (line 9)
6. split (line 10)
7. sued (line 15)

4 **Group Work** Discuss.

1. What do you think of Popov's decision to take Hayashi to court? Why?
2. Do you think the judge made the right decision? Why or why not?

Grammar | conjunctions: *both, neither, either*

5 Look at the Active Grammar box and complete the rules with *both*, *neither*, or *either*.

Active Grammar

Both men tried to catch the ball.

Neither man got all the money.

I don't think *either* man should get any money.

1. Use *both, neither,* or *either* when talking about two things or people.

 a. _____ means "one **or** the other."

 b. _____ means "one **and** the other."

 c. _____ means "**not** one and **not** the other."

2. *Both, neither,* and *either* can be followed by *of* + pronoun or (*the/these*, etc.) + noun.
 Neither of the men got the money.

See Reference page 126

6 Complete the sentences with *both*, *neither*, or *either*.

1. _____ of my two best friends is married yet.
2. _____ of my parents have always worked.
3. _____ of them is retired yet.
4. Let's see _____ a movie or a play.
5. I prefer a play, but _____ is OK with me.

Pronunciation | *both, neither,* and *either*

7a ▶2.26 Listen to the sentences in Exercise 6. How are *both, neither,* and *either* pronounced?

b **Pair Work** Take turns saying the sentences in Exercise 6 aloud.

Speaking

8a **Pair Work** Find four things you have in common with another student. Think about:

food	going shopping
sports	arts and entertainment
travel	spending/borrowing/lending/saving money

b Tell another student what you learned.

> First, **both** of us like going shopping, but **neither** of us is very good at saving money.

Extra Listening Activity in *ACTIVEBOOK*

Review

1   Complete the unreal conditional sentences with the correct forms of the verbs.

Ex: We __would move__ (move) to the country if our jobs __weren't__ (not be) in the city.

1. If I _____ (have) some money, I _____ (buy) this CD.
2. My job _____ (be) much easier if I _____ (speak) Spanish.
3. If he _____ (get) up earlier, he _____ (not be) late for work.
4. I _____ (feel) happier if my daughter _____ (call) more often.
5. If you _____ (not work) so hard, you _____ (not be) so tired.
6. I _____ (take) an art course if I _____ (have) more time.
7. If I _____ (find) a wallet in the street, I _____ (take) it to a police station.

2   Circle the correct choice to complete each sentence.

Ex: He _said_/*told* the police nothing.

1. They didn't _say/tell_ Peter that I was at home.
2. She _said/told_ him to go.
3. Why did you _say/tell_ that you hated your job?
4. Nobody _said/told_ that the station was closed for a month.
5. You shouldn't _say/tell_ you want to quit if you don't mean it.
6. Who _said/told_ you that I was with Carmen?
7. She didn't _say/tell_ them she was getting married.

3   **Pair Work** Say the opposite of what your partner says first. Take turns replying.

Ex: **A:** Tim likes chocolate.

   B: I thought you said Tim didn't like chocolate!

1. **A:** I'm going home soon.
   B: I thought you said . . .
2. **A:** We'll see Steve and Jim tomorrow.
   B: I thought you said . . .
3. **A:** I don't have much time right now.
   B: I thought you said . . .

4. **A:** They borrowed my car for the weekend.
   B: I thought you said . . .
5. **A:** I've talked to Tara.
   B: I thought you said . . .

4   Read the following sentences and decide if *both*, *neither*, or *either* is used correctly. If not, correct the sentence.

Ex: Neither of them wanted to do the dishes. *OK*

1. Both of men were wearing long black coats.
2. Neither hotels has a swimming pool.
3. I was invited to two parties last weekend, but I didn't go to either of them.
4. I think that both candidates for the job are very good.
5. I'm afraid the math teacher has had problems with either of your sons.
6. I don't think I like neither of her brothers.
7. I can't believe it. She invited both of her ex-boyfriends to the party!

5 Match the sentences below to one of the pictures.

_____ 1. I'd like to speak to someone about this sweater.

_____ 2. Excuse me, I think there's a mistake with the bill.

_____ 3. I'm sorry, but I gave you a $20 bill.

_____ 4. We actually had only two coffees, not three.

_____ 5. Well, the first time I washed it, the color came out.

_____ 6. I should have $14.60 in change, not $4.60.

_____ 7. I'm very sorry, ma'am. I'll take it off the bill.

_____ 8. You're right. Here's the correct change.

_____ 9. Can I ask what temperature you washed it at?

6 ▶2.27 Listen to three conversations and check your answers to Exercise 5.

7a Listen again. Write down the main points of each conversation as you listen.

b **Group Work** Work in groups of three. Use reported speech to tell about the conversations.

Student A: report Conversation 1   **Student C:** report Conversation 3
Student B: report Conversation 2

> *First, the customer told the waiter that there was a mistake with the bill. Then . . .*

8 **Pair Work** Practice roleplaying the conversations. Take turns being the customer. First, the store clerk or waiter should be helpful. Then, he or she should be less helpful.

Unit 12 Reference

Unreal conditional

Use the unreal conditional to talk about unlikely or imagined situations in the present or future.

Form: *If* + simple past, *would* (or *'d*) + verb
> *If I won some money, I'd go to Australia.*

The *if* clause can come first or second.
> *I'd train to be a pilot if I weren't afraid of flying.*

When we are less certain, we can use *might* instead of *would*.
> *If I had more money, I might buy some new clothes.*

Compare with the real conditional, which we use for talking about possible situations in the future.
> *If I pass all my tests, I will go out to celebrate.*

Reported speech

Use reported or indirect speech to tell people what somebody said or thought.

Make the tense of the verb one "step" further back into the past.

Direct Speech	Indirect reported speech
"I **have** $50."	He said (that) he **had** $50.
"Janice **is living** in Ecuador."	She said (that) Janice **was living** in Ecuador.
"She **went** home."	He said (that) she **had gone** home.
"He **has worked** there since March."	He said (that) she **had worked** there since March.
"I'm sure **she'll pass** the test."	He said he was sure she s**would pass** the test.

If somebody said something that is still true when it is reported, tenses don't always change.
> *"I don't like carrots."*
> *She said that she doesn't like carrots.*

Say or *tell* are often used in reported speech. *Tell* must have an object. We *tell* somebody something. *That* is often left out.
> *She said she saw Gordon on Friday.*
> *She told me she saw Gordon on Friday.*

A change of speaker may mean a change of pronoun.
> *"We don't like Tony."*
> *She said that they didn't like Tony.*

Conjunctions: *both, neither, either*

Use *both*, *neither*, and *either* to talk about two people or things. For example:
> *Both jackets are expensive.*
> *Neither jacket fits me very well.*
> *I don't like either jacket.*

Use *both* with a plural noun. It means one and the other.

Use *neither* with a singular noun. It means not one and not the other.

Use *either* with a singular noun. It means one or the other.

When you use *both/neither/either* + *of*, you also need *the* or *these/those* or *my/your/his*, etc. If a noun follows, it must be plural.
> *Both of my sisters are in college.*
> *Neither of them is married.*
> *I haven't seen either of them for ages.*

You can use *both . . . and*.
> *He's both intelligent and good-looking.*

Neither is usually used instead of *both . . . not*.
> *Neither of them came to the meeting.*

For the negative, use *neither . . . nor.* (formal)
> *He speaks neither Japanese nor Chinese.*

Unit Vocabulary

Money

lend	borrow	earn a salary
save	withdraw	pay with cash
earn	pay taxes	get a pension
spend	pay interest	

Other vocabulary

stands (n)	take to court
official	split
grab	sue
end up	

Speaking Exchange

Unit 2 | Page 22, Exercise 2a
Student A

- He sings Latin dance and pop music.
- He has released over nine albums.
- He has released Spanish, English, and bilingual albums.
- He has won one Grammy award and one Latin Grammy award.
- He has acted in one movie. He was in *Once Upon a Time in Mexico* with Salma Hayek, Antonio Banderas, and Johnny Depp.
- He has never been married, but he has dated actresses, singers, and a Russian tennis star.
- He was born in 1975 in Madrid, but he grew up in Miami.
- His father is Spanish and his mother is Filipino. His father is a very famous singer.
- His name is Enrique Iglesias.

Unit 3 | Page 31, Exercise 8
Student A

Explain these words to your partner. Your partner listens and says the word you are describing.

knife	pilot	tea	ice cream
plate	stove	salt	

Unit 8 | Page 83, Exercise 6a
Student A's

Read the information below.

A large number of diamonds were stolen from a store in your town between 9:00 and 11:00 last night. Both of you are suspects. The police are going to interview you separately about what you were doing during that time.

In order to convince them that you are not the thieves, you need to prove that you were together during that time. You will need to tell them exactly the same things about what you were doing.

Prepare what you are going to say; for example: *what you were wearing, what you were doing between those times, where you went, who you were with.*

Get ready to be interviewed. Try and keep your stories the same.

Unit 9 | Page 95, Exercise 6a
Group A

You have worked for a small family company for two years. The company sells books over the Internet. You have worked hard for a small salary. Now you and your eight co-workers feel that conditions need to improve.

YOUR GOALS

- **increase salaries**
  - by 6–7% (5 points)
  - by 4–5% (3 points)
  - by 2–3% (1 point)
- **increase number of vacation days per year (currently 10)**
  - by 6–8 days (5 points)
  - by 4–5 days (3 points)
  - by 2–3 days (1 point)
- **reduce weekly hours (currently 40 hours a week)**
  - by 4–5 hours (5 points)
  - by 2–3 hours (3 points)
  - by 1 hour (1 point)
- **introduce benefits for staff: free lunch, free coffee, and cheap books**
  - all three benefits (5 points)
  - two of the benefits (3 points)
  - one of the benefits (1 point)

Unit 9 | Page 93, Exercise 8b

Group A

Begin your story like this: Four men were visiting London . . .

Unit 1 | Page 13, Exercise 8

Student B

Unit 2 | Page 22, Exercise 2a

Student B

- He sings mostly salsa music.
- He has released over 12 albums.
- He has released both Spanish and English language albums.
- He has won 4 Grammy awards and 3 Latin Grammy awards.
- He has been in ten movies. He recently starred in a movie with his wife.
- He has been married twice. His first wife was a model and actress, and his second wife is a very famous singer and movie star.
- He was born in 1968 in New York City.
- His parents were Puerto Rican Americans.
- His name is Marc Anthony.

Unit 3 | Page 31, Exercise 8

Student B

Explain these words to your partner. Your partner listens and says the word you are describing.

sugar	pepper	soup	doctor
bowl	fridge	fork	

Unit 11 | Page 115, Exercise 7b
Student A

1 You are buying a ticket at Penn Station in New York. Your partner is a clerk in a ticket booth. Before you buy your ticket, read the information below.

> You want a one-way ticket to Washington, D.C. You'd like the least expensive ticket on a train leaving soon. You want to pay by debit card.

2 Now change roles. You are a clerk in a ticket booth at Penn Station. Your partner is a customer. Use the information below.

TICKETS TO BOSTON
Prices:

Acela Express one way: $111   roundtrip: $222
Northeast Regional one way: $64   roundtrip: $128

Next Train:

Acela Express leaves 8:03   arrives 11:32
Northeast Regional leaves 8:30   arrives 12:48

Platform:

Acela Express track 7   Northeast Regional track 12

Unit 9 | Page 89, Exercise 6

a Look at the three job ads and choose one.

b Think about these things:

Student A
1. Why would you be good for the job?
2. What experience, education, or skills do you have?
3. Why do you want the job?
4. What questions might the interviewer ask you?
5. What questions do you want to ask the interviewer?

Student B
1. What does the job involve?
2. What kind of person do you want?
3. What questions are you going to ask the interviewee?
4. What questions might the interviewee ask you?

c Student B: Interview Student A. Tell Student A if he or she got the job or not. Give reasons.

Unit 9 | Page 95, Exercise 6a
Group B

You own and run a small family company that sells books over the Internet. You employ nine people. You started the company two years ago. After a difficult start, things are beginning to look more positive, but the future is still very uncertain.

YOUR GOALS
- **avoid big salary increases for staff**
  - salaries stay the same (5 points)
  - salary increase of 1–2% (3 points)
  - salary increase of 3–4% (1 point)
- **avoid big increase in number of vacation days per year (currently 10)**
  - no increase (5 points)
  - increase by 1 day (3 points)
  - increase by 2 days (1 point)
- **increase weekly hours (currently 40 hours a week)**
  - by 4–5 hours (5 points)
  - by 2–3 hours (3 points)
  - by 1 hour (1 point)
- **no benefits for staff: no free lunch, no free coffee, and no cheap books**
  - no benefits for staff (5 points)
  - one benefit for staff (3 points)
  - two benefits for staff (1 point)

HARBARD UNIVERSITY DEPARTMENT OF LANGUAGES
is looking for foreign students to provide one-on-one speaking practice to university students learning foreign languages.

The International School of English
Receptionist wanted to deal with inquiries, give information, and enroll students.

Horizon Children's Summer School
Requires enthusiastic helpers to supervise groups (6–15) during afternoon activities (sports, drama, etc.) this summer.

Unit 11 | Page 110, Exercise 2a

Group B

2a Read the article below.

ADVICE FOR BUSINESS TRAVELERS

Forms of address

In most countries, business people use their last names when they talk to each other. In some countries (Germany and Switzerland, for example), business people use last names even when they know each other well. To be safe, continue using someone's last name until he or she asks you to use his or her first name.

Personal space

People in South America and southern Europe stand quite close to each other when talking—about 60 centimeters apart—while in the Middle East they sometimes stand even closer—less than 30 centimeters apart. People from northern Europe and the US stand further apart and feel uncomfortable if you stand too close. Their preferred distance is 75 to 90 centimeters apart.

Physical greetings

In most countries, people shake hands when they meet in business situations. You should be careful that your handshake is not too strong or too weak. In Asia, the main form of greeting is the bow. When greeting Westerners, many Asians follow the bow with a handshake. Even in countries where it is common to kiss (Italy and Russia, for example), it is usually only for people who know each other well.

b Work with a student who read article A. Answer your partner's questions. Then ask your partner these questions.

1. When should you give presents in Japan?
2. What kind of gift should you give in Japan?
3. Is it OK to give four flowers in Japan?
4. Is it OK to give clocks in China?
5. Why should you be careful with leather products in South America?
6. Is it always OK to give red flowers in Europe?

Unit 11 | Page 115, Exercise 7b

Student B

1 You are a clerk in a ticket booth at Penn Station in New York. Your partner is a customer. Use the information below.

TICKETS TO WASHINGTON, DC

Prices:

Acela Express one way: $180   roundtrip: $360
Northeast Regional one way: $127   roundtrip: $254

Next Train:

Acela Express leaves 2:00   arrives 4:47
Northeast Regional leaves 2:05   arrives 5:20

Platform:

Acela Express track 18   Northeast Regional track 6

2 Now change roles. You are buying a ticket at Penn Station. Your partner is a clerk. Before you buy your ticket, read the information below.

You want a round-trip ticket to Boston. You want to get there as quickly as possible on a train leaving soon. You want to pay with cash.

Unit 7 | Page 75, Exercise 6b

Total Stress Factor

10–15: You are one cool customer who is always calm under pressure. Well done!

16–25: Not bad . . . you're mostly stress-free—just a little tense sometimes!

26–35: Keep an eye on yourself. You are nearly at dangerous levels of stress . . . don't go there!

36–50: Watch out! You are getting too stressed, too often. You need to keep calm before you go completely crazy!

Unit 6 | Page 59, Exercise 7

Discuss:

1. What are some interesting tourist attractions in your region? How would you describe them to a tourist from another country?

2. Which tourist attraction is a "must see" for a tourist?

3. What do you think the future of tourism in your region will be like? Why?

4. Work with another pair. Discuss your answers to these questions.

Unit 2 | Page 22, Exercise 2a

Student C

- He sings Latin pop music.
- He has released over ten albums.
- He has released albums mainly in Spanish.
- He has won 2 Grammy awards and 15 Latin Grammy awards.
- He has not starred in any movies, but he has been in a lot of music videos.
- He is single. He has been married once and has two children.
- He was born in 1968 in Madrid.
- His parents are Spanish. His father is a musician.
- His name is Alejandro Sanz.

Unit 8 | Page 83, Exercise 6a

Student B's

Read the information below.

A large number of diamonds were stolen from a store in your town between 9:00 and 11:00 last night. Both of you are police officers. You are going to interview two suspects separately about what they were doing during that time.

In order to try and prove that one of them committed this crime, you need to show that they are lying about the fact that they were together during this time. You will need to get as much detail as possible and then afterwards compare their stories.

Prepare what you are going to ask; for example, *What were you wearing? Where did you go first? Did you meet anyone?*

Get ready to interview the suspects. Then decide if they are guilty—are their stories the same?

Unit 9 | Page 93, Exercise 8b

Group B

Begin your story like this: Three men tried to rob a bank . . .

Unit 10 | Page 103, Exercise 6b

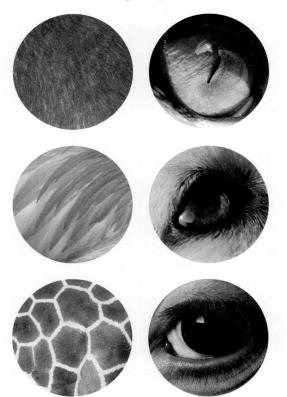

Unit 11 | Page 108, Exercise 5

Say what Lucy's *just done*, *has already done*, and what she *hasn't done yet*, using the words in the box.

fold/clothes	pack/bag
wash/hair	dry/hair
make/bed	brush/teeth
have/shower	write/postcards

Writing Bank

Unit 1 | Page 13, Exercise 9

Informal email

1 Read the email below and circle the answer to these questions.

1. What is Gaby describing?
- **a.** her life now
- **b.** her plans for the future

2. What does Gaby ask Enrico?
- **a.** to come and stay
- **b.** to write her an email

Hi Enrico,

> Informal language for greeting, for example, *Hi Enrico*; *Hello Enrico*; *Dear Enrico*

① I've got so much to tell you. Things are different for me now. I'm living in Canada now! We're here for a year.

② James is working for a bank in Vancouver and I'm studying at the film school. We're staying in an apartment in the center of town. There are lots of things to do in the city, but every weekend we go to the country. It's really beautiful!

③ What about you? I'd love to know what you're doing these days. Send me an email soon.

Love, Gaby xxx

> Informal language for ending, for example, *Love, Gaby*; *Lots of love, Gaby*; *All the best, Gaby*

Useful Phrases

Give general news	*I have so much/a lot of news to tell you.* *We're living in Canada!*
Giving news in detail	*I'm working at a bank.* *We're studying medicine.* *I go into the city every weekend.*
Ask about your friend	*I'd love to know what you're doing.* *It would be great to hear from you.* *Please write/email me soon.*

Writing skill | paragraphs

2 Match these descriptions to paragraphs 1–3 in the email.

____ **a.** asking to hear about your friend's life

____ **b.** saying generally what you are doing

____ **c.** saying in detail what you are doing

Unit 3 | Page 31, Exercise 9

Informal invitation

1 Read the email and answer the questions.

1. Why hasn't Steve written to Sophie before now?

2. What is his main reason for writing to Sophie now?

3. What does Steve want Sophie to do?

Hi Sophie,

> Introduction. Say what you have done recently

Thanks a lot for your message. I'm sorry I didn't reply sooner, but I've been on vacation in Italy. I had a wonderful time and want to show you all my photos when I see you!

Anyway, I was wondering if you'd like to come to a small dinner party at my house on June 23rd at 8 P.M. Sam and Julie will be there and two other friends that you don't know. Let me know if you can come. I hope you can!

> Explain reason for writing

Looking forward to seeing you very soon.

> Closing. Say when you will next be in touch

Love, Steve

(continued on next page)

Unit 3 Writing skill |
starting/ending letters

2 Mark these salutations and closings as formal (*F*) or informal (*I*).

____ Dear Sarah,

____ Dear Sir or Madam:

____ Dear Mr. Davies,

____ Yours faithfully,

____ Love,

____ Best wishes,

____ Sincerely,

Useful Phrases

Introduction	• *Thanks a lot for your letter.* • *It was really nice to hear from you.*
Explain the reason for writing	• *The reason I'm writing is . . .* • *I was wondering if you . . .*
Conclusion	• *Write back soon and tell me your news.* • *Hope everything's OK with you.* • *Looking forward to seeing you soon.* • *Give my love to your family.*

Unit 12 | Page 121, Exercise 7a

Formal letter

1 Read the letter and answer these questions.

1. Why is Alberto writing this letter?
2. What three things does he want to know?

Writing skill | sequencers

2 Put the following words and phrases into three groups of similar meaning.

> to start with   first   second
> to begin with   next   finally
> in addition   last
> I'd also like to know

> How to start a formal letter to an unknown person

> Your address

> Recipient's address

> Introduction: Explain how you know about the person/company and the reason for writing

> Explain exactly what information you would like

> How to end a letter beginning "Dear Sir or Madam"

Blvd. Patrotas
Colonia Roma
México City 42811
México

Austin School of English
300 West 10th Street
Austin, TX 78705

April 12, 2011

Dear Sir or Madam:

I recently saw your advertisement for Summer Intensive Courses and would like some more information.

First, can you tell me the specific dates of the courses during July and August? Second, do you know how many students there will be in the classes?

Finally, can you tell me if you arrange accommodation with local families, or is that something I have to do myself?

Sincerely,

Alberto Garcia Ramirez

Useful Phrases

Explain the reason for writing	• *I recently saw your advertisement in* The New York Times. • *I'd be grateful if you could send me some information about your courses.*
Ask for the exact information you need	• *Could you tell me how long the course lasts?* • *Could you send me a brochure about the courses your college offers?*

Unit 6 | Page 63, Exercise 7

Description

1 Read the description and answer these questions.

    1. What is special about the trees in Oak Hills?

    2. Why does the writer like Oak Hills when the weather is hot?

    3. In which season does the writer prefer to be in the woods?

    4. Does the writer live in a place that is similar to or different from Oak Hills?

Writing skill |
referencing words

2 Find these <u>underlined</u> words in the description and say what they refer to.

    1. them (line 3):

    2. there (line 4):

    3. It (line 5):

    4. it (line 6):

    5. It (line 11):

    6. there (line 14):

Unit 8 | Page 83, Exercise 7

Short story

1 Read the story. Then circle the correct choice to complete each sentence.

    1. The writer went for a walk *with his cousin/on his own*.

    2. He didn't know the way *to his cousin's house/to the top of the mountain*.

    3. The dog *was very quiet/made a lot of noise*.

    4. The writer *followed/took* the dog to his cousin's house.

    5. The dog *stayed/didn't stay* with the writer.

What/Where your favorite place is

One of my favorite natural places is a nature area near where I live called Oak Hills. Many of the trees are very old—some of <u>them</u> have been <u>there</u> for hundreds of years.

5 <u>It</u> is a beautiful place to go in every season, whatever the weather. When <u>It's</u> very hot, you can keep cool under the trees. I also like walking in the woods in the rain. My favorite time to go is fall, when the leaves are incredible colors—red, 10 orange, yellow, and gold.

Oak Hills is a very special place for me. <u>It</u> is an escape from the noisy, crowded city I live in. <u>It's</u> beautiful and peaceful, and I always feel better when I go <u>there</u>.

Gabriela Pisani

Why you like it/what you do there

Summarize why it's special for you

Useful Phrases

Say what/where your favorite place is	• *One of my favorite natural places is . . .* • *One place that is very special to me is . . .*
Say why you like it/ what you do there	• *It's a beautiful place to go in the fall . . .* • *I like/My favorite time to go there is in the early morning/when it's snowing . . .* • *When it's very hot/cold/wet, you can . . .*
Summarize why it's special for you	• *It's an escape from the city/stress/work . . .* • *I feel happy and relaxed when I'm there.*

Use narrative tenses

It all happened last summer. I was staying at my cousin's house in the mountains, and I was
① bored. I really wanted something exciting to happen, so I decided to go for a walk alone. At first, it was sunny, the mountains, were beautiful, and I felt happy. But time passed
② quickly, and soon it was getting dark. I realized that I was a long way from my cousin's house and I was completely lost!

Suddenly, I heard a strange noise and saw a large dog. He was barking, and he seemed to be asking me to go with him. So I decided to
③ follow him. After a while, he took me to my cousin's house. He ran off into the night, and I never saw him again.

Use interesting vocabulary

Use phrases to show when things happened.

(continued on next page)

Writing skill | organizing your story

2   Match these descriptions to paragraphs 1–3 in the story on page 135.

   ____ a. Describe the main events of the story, for example, a problem, a crime, or a mystery.

   ____ b. Set the scene, including the place, the person/people, and the feelings.

   ____ c. Say what happens in the end. Remember that an interesting ending is the most important part of your story.

Useful Phrases

Set the scene	• It all happened last summer/ during my last vacation . . . • One day/morning/night . . . • I was staying at . . .
Describe the main events of the story	• At first, . . ./To begin with, . . . • After a while, . . . /Soon, . . . • Suddenly, . . . • Finally, . . ./In the end, . . .
Show when things happened	• Time passed quickly and . . . • I realized that . . . • So I decided to . . .

Unit 10 | Page 101, Exercise 5

Blogs

1   Read the blog and mark the statements true (*T*) or false (*F*).

   ____ 1. Paula doesn't think it is necessary to take anything.

   ____ 2. Craig disagrees with Paula.

   ____ 3. Craig will always take flowers.

   ____ 4. Kelly will take different things for different people. It depends on how well she knows them.

Useful Phrases

IMO—In my opinion	K—OK
W/O—Without	LOL—Laugh out loud
BTW—By the way	ur—You are
B4N—Bye for now	u2—You, too

MODERN DAY POLITENESS BLOG

Post responses to the question:

What should you take when you are invited for dinner?

Paula: IMO, you don't have to take anything. If I invite people for dinner, it's because I want to see them, not because I expect anything!

Craig: I would never arrive for dinner W/O a small gift! I usually take something to drink and maybe flowers.

Kelly: I think it all depends on who you're visiting. With really good friends who I see a lot, I probably wouldn't take anything . . . But if it's more formal, or people I don't know very well, then I'd do the same as Craig—something to drink and flowers are always appreciated.

Writing skill | its/it's

Its (without apostrophe) is a possessive adjective. *It's* (with apostrophe) is a contraction.

2   Find and correct the mistakes with *its* in these sentences.

   1. If I invite people to dinner, *its* because I want to see them.

   2. I think you should give the dog *its* food now.

   3. Every family has *its* own special way of celebrating this holiday.

   4. We're late for the movie. I'm afraid *its* started already.

Pronunciation Bank

Part 1 | ▶ 2.28 English phonemes

Part 2 | ▶ 2.29 Sound-spelling correspondences

Consonants

Symbol	Key word	Symbol	Key word
d	**d**ate	ŋ	goi**ng**
b	**b**ed	s	**s**ofa
t	**t**en	z	**z**ero
p	**p**ark	ʃ	**sh**op
k	**c**ar	ʒ	televi**si**on
g	**g**ame	h	**h**at
tʃ	**ch**ild	m	**m**enu
dʒ	**j**ob	n	**n**ear
f	**f**our	l	**l**ike
v	**v**isit	r	**r**ide
θ	**th**ree	y	**y**oung
ð	**th**is	w	**w**ife

Vowels

Symbol	Key word	Symbol	Key word
i	b**e**	ə	**a**bout
ɪ	s**i**t	eɪ	d**ay**
ɛ	r**e**d	aɪ	b**y**
æ	c**a**t	aʊ	h**ou**se
ɑ	f**a**ther	ɔɪ	b**oy**
oʊ	b**oa**t	ɑr	**car**
ɔ	b**ough**t	ɔr	d**oor**
ʊ	b**oo**k	ʊr	t**our**
u	sh**oe**	ɪr	h**ere**
ʌ	b**u**t	ɛr	th**ere**
ɚ	w**or**d		

Sound	Spelling	Examples
/ɪ/	i	this listen
	y	gym typical
	ui	build guitar
	e	pretty
/i/	ee	green sleep
	ie	niece believe
	ea	read teacher
	e	these complete
	ey	key money
	ei	receipt receive
	i	police
/æ/	a	can man land
/ɑ/	a	pasta
	al	calm
	ea	heart
/ʌ/	u	fun sunny husband
	o	some mother month
	ou	cousin double young
/ɔ/	ou	bought
	au	daughter taught
	al	bald small always
	aw	draw jigsaw
/aɪ/	i	like time island
	y	dry shy cycle
	ie	fries die tie
	igh	light high right
	ei	height
	ey	eyes
	uy	buy
/ɛɪ/	a	lake hate shave
	ai	wait train straight
	ay	play say stay
	ey	they obey
	ei	eight weight
	ea	break
/oʊ/	o	home phone open
	ow	show throw own
	oa	coat road coast
	ol	cold told

Part 3 | ▶ 2.30 Silent consonants

Some letters appear in words where they are not pronounced.

Letter	Silent in:	Letter	Silent in:	Letter	Silent in:
b	dou**b**t clim**b**	h	**h**our w**h**at	p	**p**sychology recei**p**t
c	s**c**issors s**c**ene	k	**k**now **k**nee	s	i**s**land ai**s**le
d	We**d**nesday san**d**wich	l	ta**l**k ca**l**m	t	lis**t**en whis**t**le
g	ou**g**ht lon**g**	n	autum**n** colum**n**	w	**w**rite ans**w**er

Irregular Verbs

Verb	Simple Past	Past Participle
be	was/were	been
become	became	become
begin	began	begun
break	broke	broken
bring	brought	brought
build	built	built
buy	bought	bought
can	could	been able
catch	caught	caught
choose	chose	chosen
come	came	come
cost	cost	cost
dig	dug	dug
do	did	done
draw	drew	drawn
drink	drank	drunk
drive	drove	driven
eat	ate	eaten
fall	fell	fallen
feed	fed	fed
feel	felt	felt
find	found	found
fly	flew	flown
forget	forgot	forgotten
get	got	gotten
give	gave	given
go	went	gone/been
grow	grew	grown
have	had	had
hear	heard	heard
hold	held	held
hurt	hurt	hurt
keep	kept	kept
know	knew	known
learn	learned	learned

Verb	Simple Past	Past Participle
leave	left	left
let	let	let
lose	lost	lost
make	made	made
mean	meant	meant
meet	met	met
pay	paid	paid
put	put	put
read/rid/	read/rɛd/	read/rɛd/
ride	rode	ridden
ring	rang	rung
run	ran	run
say	said	said
see	saw	seen
sell	sold	sold
send	sent	sent
shine	shone	shone
show	showed	shown
sing	sang	sung
sit	sat	sat
sleep	slept	slept
speak	spoke	spoken
spend	spent	spent
stand	stood	stood
steal	stole	stolen
swim	swam	swum
take	took	taken
teach	taught	taught
tell	told	told
think	thought	thought
throw	threw	thrown
understand	understood	understood
wear	wore	worn
win	won	won
write	wrote	written

Audioscript

UNIT 1 Your day

▶ **1.02** (Page 10)

M: Everybody knows that cats like sleeping . . . they spend half their lives asleep and enjoy every minute of it. Other animals have very different sleeping habits, however. These horses may not look like they are asleep. But they are! Horses only spend about three hours sleeping every day, and they do it standing up! Fish sleep for about seven hours a day, but they too have strange habits . . . they don't close their eyes to sleep.

So, what about us? Well, most people sleep for about a third of their lives. The number of hours you actually sleep, however, depends on your age. Newborn babies sleep a lot—usually about 17 hours out of every 24. That's nearly 75% of their time spent asleep! As we get older we need less sleep. Children need about eleven hours, and adults sleep for about eight hours every night. So, yes, on average you spend about 2,688 hours a year doing nothing—asleep in bed!

But you're not just asleep—you're not really doing nothing. Your body and your mind rest during this time, but a lot happens during sleep. Dreams are one way that the mind rests after a busy day. The average person spends about 20% of every night dreaming. That means you have about four or five dreams every night, or about 1,800 dreams a year.

▶ **1.05** (Page 12)

Person 1

F1: Excuse me. We're doing interviews today. Can I ask you a few questions?
F2: Sure, no problem.
F1: Are you a New Yorker, or are you visiting?
F2: I'm visiting. I'm from Brazil.
F1: And what are you doing in New York?
F2: I'm visiting my sister for a few weeks. I have summer vacation now, and I'm helping her take care of her kids. And, of course, seeing New York.
F1: And what are you doing at Tiffany's?
F2: I'm just looking. I love this store, but everything is pretty expensive, so I'm not buying anything today. But I love looking!
F1: All right. Sounds fun. Thanks very much.

Person 2

F1: Excuse me. Can I ask you a few questions?
M1: Um, yeah, OK.
F1: First, where are you from?
M1: I'm from Mexico City, Mexico.
F1: Great. And what are you doing in New York?
M1: I'm here on vacation with my girlfriend. We're not staying long—just three days.
F1: OK. And are you looking for anything special at Tiffany's?

M1: Well, yes. My girlfriend is shopping for clothes right now, and this is a secret, but I'm looking for an engagement ring for her.
F1: An engagement ring? That's great!
M1: Maybe you could help me? Could you come in and tell me which ring you like?
F1: Well, I'm sorry, but . . . Good luck with that!

Person 3

F1: Excuse me, ma'am. Can I ask you a few questions?
F3: Oh, well, yes, all right.
F1: Um, first, where are you from?
F3: I live here in New York, of course. We have a penthouse on the Upper East Side.
F1: Oh, OK. And what are you doing today?
F3: I'm shopping, my dear. Shopping is wonderful, isn't it? So much fun.
F1: And what are you shopping for at Tiffany's?
F3: Well, to tell you the truth, I'm trying to find some jewelry for a big party this weekend. Something new. A new necklace, some earrings. I'm here with a friend, and we like to go shopping for jewelry together. We'll go to Tiffany's, Harry Winston, Cartier . . . It may take a day or two to find the perfect thing.
F1: Ah, well um, I wish you the best of luck!
F3: Thank you, my dear. Same to you.

▶ **1.07** (Page 15)

M1: OK . . . I finished my wheel . . . can I tell you about it?
F1: Yes, of course. Go ahead.
M1: Well, let's start with grammar. Grammar is pretty important to me, so I've put three for that.
F1: And you're good at grammar, aren't you?
M1: Yes, I am.
F1: What about vocabulary?
M1: Well, I've put four for that because it's important to me. But I think I need to improve my vocabulary, because I'm not very good at remembering new words.
F1: OK. So . . . reading?
M1: Well, three for reading—it's pretty important to me, and I'm pretty good at reading generally, so I feel happy about that . . .
F1: Are you good at listening too?
M1: Pardon?
F1: Very funny.
M1: I'm not very good at listening, because people usually speak so fast. But I put four for that, because it's very important to me. I really need to practice more.
F1: Is speaking important to you?
M1: Yes, it's very important. I've put five for speaking and pronunciation. I need more practice, because I'm pretty good, but I'd like to be more fluent.
F1: And the last one . . . what about writing?
M1: Well, I'm good at writing, but it's not very important. I don't need to write in English much . . . just two for that . . .
F1: Two for writing . . . OK . . . Can I tell you about my wheel now?

UNIT 2 Musical tastes

▶ **1.08** (Page 18)

F: Lady Gaga's real name is Stefani Germanotta. She was born in 1986 in Yonkers, a suburb of New York City. She began learning to play the piano when she was 4, and began performing at age 14. Although her parents weren't rich, she went to a private school in New York City. As a high school student, she loved both the theater and singing. In fact, she played the lead roles in two high school musicals. Although she was a good student, she said that she "didn't fit in" and "felt like a freak" at school. At the age of 17, Stefani began studying music at New York University. A year and a half later, she left school to focus on her singing career. She began working as a waitress and performing in New York's Lower East Side clubs. She changed her name to Lady Gaga at this time, and got a job with Sony/ATV. For Sony/ATV, she wrote songs for Britney Spears and other pop singers. Then in 2008, she moved to Los Angeles and finished recording her first album. The album, *The Fame*, was a huge success all over the world.

▶ **1.10** (Page 21)

relaxed
relaxation
energetic
energy
imaginative
imagination
intelligent
intelligence

▶ **1.11** (Page 23)

M1: Have you ever won a competition?
F1: Yes, I have. I won a singing competition when I was six.
F1: Did you watch TV last night?
M1: Yes, I did. I saw a documentary about global warming.
M1: Have you ever met a famous person?
F1: No, I haven't. But I saw Madonna in concert last year!
F1: Have you ever played a musical instrument in public?
M1: Yes, I have. I was in a band when I was a teenager.

▶ **1.12** (Page 25)

F1: On *My Top Three* today, we're talking to actor Ben Parker. What are his top three records? Imagine he is alone on a desert island for ten weeks. Which music would he want? Which three pieces of music would he take with him to this desert island? Let's talk to him and find out. Hello Ben—welcome to *My Top Three*.
M1: Hello, it's great to be here.
F1: So, imagine—you're going to be alone on a desert island. You can take only three pieces of music. Which three do you want? First . . . tell us about number three . . .

▶ 1.13 (Page 25)

M1: Well, it's pretty hard to choose—but I think number three for me is "Dancing Queen" by Abba. I love it!

F1: Really!

M1: It reminds me of when I was in college. My roommate was really into Abba. This music makes me feel great. I always want to dance when I hear it!

F1: Cool! . . . so number three is Abba, what about number two?

M1: Number two is something totally different . . . it's a piece of classical music. It brings back great memories for me. I first heard it when I was about ten years old, though I didn't know anything about classical music back then. It's the fourth movement of Mahler's Symphony number five. When I first heard it, it made me cry because it was so beautiful!! I still love it.

F1: Yeah . . . So, number one . . . what's your all-time number one favorite piece of music?

M1: Well, I think my favorite song ever is "Bridge Over Troubled Water," by Simon and Garfunkel. Their voices harmonize so perfectly. Whenever I'm feeling anxious or stressed out, playing this song helps me relax. It also brings back great memories—I remember listening to this song when I was on vacation in Spain.

F1: Oh, I love that song, too! Thanks for coming in today to tell us about your top three, Ben . . .

▶ 1.14 (Page 25)

1. It reminds me of when I was in college.
2. This music makes me feel great.
3. When I first heard it, it made me cry because it was so beautiful!
4. I remember listening to this song when I was on vacation in Spain.

UNIT 3 Fine cuisine

▶ 1.15 (Page 29)

Interviewer: . . . So have you enjoyed working in a restaurant in a big hotel?

Girl: Yes, it's been great. And I've been working for a top chef. I've learned a lot, but my contract finishes at the end of this month.

Interviewer: So what are you going to do next?

Girl: Well, my dad has a friend who runs a small restaurant in the south of France. I'm going to work for him over the summer.

Interviewer: Wow . . . lucky you! Just the summer?

Girl: Yeah, but that's OK. I'm not going to stay there longer than a few months because what I really want to do is get a job in the States . . .

▶ 1.16 (Page 30)

M1: So did you do much yesterday?

F1: No, not really. I just stayed home and watched a video.

M1: Was it any good?

F1: Yeah, actually, it was great. *Big Night*—do you know it?

M1: I think I've heard of it, I'm not sure . . .

F1: Well, it's set in the US in the 1950s, and it's about two Italian brothers who live in New York. They own an Italian restaurant that isn't doing very well. The brothers want to serve the very best Italian cooking. But, the big problem is that the customers just want spaghetti and meatballs, so they don't get many customers, and they don't have much money left!

M1: OK . . .

F1: Well, next door, there's a restaurant where they serve terrible Italian food, but it's really popular. The brothers think the owner is their friend, but actually he isn't. He tells them that they should get a famous jazz musician to have dinner at their restaurant. The plan is that they will advertise that he's coming, and then lots of people will want to come to the restaurant. So they start to prepare for the "Big Night," and they spend their last money on the evening!

M1: So what happens? Is it a success, do they . . .

F1: I'm not going to tell. Why don't you watch it yourself!

M1: Oh no, you always do this, you . . .

▶ 1.19 (Page 33)

M1: So what are you doing tonight?

F1: Well, you'll never guess . . .

M1: What?

F1: I'm going out for dinner with Carlos.

M1: Really? Who's Carlos?

F1: He's my brother's friend.

M1: Wow, that's exciting. Where are you meeting?

F1: At a French restaurant downtown.

M1: And your brother?

F1: Don't be silly, he's not coming with us! It's a blind date . . .

▶ 1.20 (Page 35)

M1: . . . Well, I'm renting this fantastic space . . . It's the first floor of this old factory. It's enormous . . . and I'm going to turn it into a really high-end restaurant. You know, there's almost nothing like that in this area. There are lots of fast-food chains selling burgers and stuff . . . but no really good restaurants.

I'd like to have about nine tables: three for two people, four for four people, and two for six people. Of course, we can always put them together for bigger groups.

I've also had a conversation with a local art gallery, and we're going to put up pictures by local artists for sale . . . with a new show every month.

I've been thinking about the menu, and I've decided that we're going to make it short and simple, but change it every couple of weeks. We're always going to have three starters, three main courses, and three desserts. In our opening weeks we're going to have as starters: goat cheese salad, tomato soup, and garlic mushrooms. For the main course: vegetarian pasta, grilled salmon and potatoes, and roast chicken and vegetables. Finally for dessert: apple pie with ice cream, chocolate cake, and cheesecake.

The food is going to be simple but delicious, and we hope to have a friendly, lively atmosphere. So, that's the plan. We're pretty excited . . .

UNIT 4 Survival

▶ 1.21 (Page 39)

1. My aunt gives her money to others. She is generous.
2. Ako feels sure that she will pass the test. She is confident.
3. Sarah can understand things quickly. She is intelligent.
4. Sandra always does what she says she will do. She is reliable.
5. Joe wants to be successful and powerful. He is ambitious.
6. My dad never lets anything stop him. He is determined.
7. Mei has a lot of natural ability as a writer. She is talented.

▶ 1.22 (Page 40)

M1: Good evening, and thank you for coming to this information session about the Hillside Survival School. My name's David Johnson. I started the school, and I'm the head teacher. I learned my survival skills while I was in the army, and since then I've used them all over the world.

Before starting the Hillside Survival School, I worked in other well-known survival schools. My real aim for this school is to help people discover nature and outdoor life, but also to learn and to have fun.

We offer a variety of courses, but our Basic Survival Course lasts a weekend and takes place throughout the year. This course teaches you the basic skills that you need to survive in the wilderness. During the course you'll have a lot of opportunities to practice these skills. The cost of the Basic Survival Course is $249 per person.

If you want an even bigger challenge, our Extreme Survival Course takes place between November and February, when the conditions are more difficult. This course also lasts for a weekend and costs $269 per person.

The Extreme Survival Course teaches you to survive in a cold and wet environment. The course offers you the chance to push yourself, both physically and mentally. No tents, no gas stoves, just you and the wilderness. You learn to find and prepare food and cook it over an open fire. You learn to build a shelter, and then you actually sleep in it. Most importantly, you learn a lot about yourself and how well you can cope with unexpected situations.

140

A few final practical details. You have to be at least 18 years old to enroll. The full cost of the course needs to be paid at least four weeks before the course begins. There are discounts for groups of four or more.

Well, I hope that gives you some idea of what we do. And now if there are any questions . . .

▶ 1.23 (Page 41)

1. Everest is the highest mountain in the world.
2. What is the best department store in New York?
3. This is the wettest day of the year so far.
4. This is the most boring movie I have ever seen.
5. Soccer is the most popular sport in Brazil.

▶ 1.24 (Page 42)

Conversation 1
F1:   Do you go to Carson Street?
M1:   Yep.
F1:   How much is it?
M1: $2.00.
F1:   Could you tell me when to get off?
M1:   Sure, no problem.

Conversation 2
F2:   Do you need any help?
F3:   Yes, please. Could you tell me if you have this in a size 4?
F2:   Sure. Let me go check.
F3:   Thanks.

Conversation 3
M2:   Hi. I need to go to 231 East Grant Street.
M3:   231 East Grant Street?
M2:   Yes. Do you know where that is?
M3:   Yep.

▶ 1.25 (Page 45)

F1:   So . . . Which of these do you think is the most important?
M1:   Well, I definitely think we should take the blankets to keep warm at night.
F1:   OK . . . so you think they're more important than the pocket knife?
M1:   No . . . not more important. We can have the pocket knife too, you know. We're allowed five things . . . .
F1:   That's true. So what else?
M1:   Well, we should take the matches so we can make a fire from all the wood you chop up with the pocket knife!
F1:   Very funny. But you're right—the matches are a must. How about the tent?
M1:   I'm not sure. We could make our own shelter from branches and things . . .
F1:   Well, maybe you could!
M1:   OK . . . we'll take the tent . . . and let's take the chocolate as number five—a little bit of luxury, OK?
F1:   Perfect!

UNIT 5 Life events

▶ 1.27 (Page 49)

1
M1:   . . . So then I met up with my brother and we had lunch in town.
F1:   How old is your brother?
M1:   He's 18.
F1:   Eighteen? So young.
M1:   Yes, but he's getting married in three months.
F1:   You're joking. And he's only 18? Gosh, I think 18 is way too young to get married. I mean, you don't know what you want when you're 18. You haven't really experienced life. What do you think?
M1:   Well, I'm not so sure . . .

2
M2:   When I was your age, things were different. I had to join the military!
M3:   Yes, Dad, I know.
M2:   You know, in my opinion, military service is a good thing, because it teaches you how to be self-sufficient.
M3:   But you can't even boil an egg!
M2:   Yes, but that's . . . not important. The important thing is, young people should learn some discipline. Don't you think so?
M3:   Yes, Dad, you're probably right. [resigned then suddenly brighter] Dad, can I borrow the car?

▶ 1.28 (Page 50)

F1:   I'm so glad you emailed. It's been ages since I heard from you!
M1:   I know. Well, I've been in Tokyo for almost two years. I'm teaching English there.
F1:   So are you enjoying it?
M1:   Yes, it's great. Especially since I met this woman named Emmy. We've known each other for about six months now. She works in the same school as me.
F1:   Oh! That's great . . . So, when are you both coming to Sao Paolo?

▶ 1.29 (Page 52)

F1:   Average lifespan can be very different from one country to another. The country with the longest average lifespan is Japan. Women live to 82.5 years on average, and men live to 76.2 years on average. This, of course, is much longer than the average lifespan 2,000 years ago. That was just 26 years. Now, everyone expects to have a long and happy life. By 2050, around 20% of the population will be age 65 or over.

If you would like to have a long life, there are certain things that seem to make a difference. On average, non-smokers live longer than smokers, married people live longer than single people, and pet owners live longer than non-pet owners. So the message is don't smoke, get married, and get a dog.

▶ 1.30 (Page 53)

1. I used to have long hair, but now it's short.
2. I didn't use to like olives, but now I do.

▶ 1.31 (Page 55)

M1:   Welcome to Biography Break—everything you want to know about your favorite people. Today we are looking at the life of actor Johnny Depp. John Christopher Depp was born in Kentucky in 1963. Because of his father's work, his family moved over 20 times. As a child, he used to feel a lot of stress, and at the age of 12 began smoking, experimenting with drugs, and hurting himself. He also began playing the guitar around this time.

When he was 15, his parents divorced, and at age 16, he dropped out of high school. He began playing guitar for a band called The Kids, and at the age of 20 moved to Los Angeles with the band. That year he also married a make-up artist. Her ex-boyfriend was the actor Nicholas Cage, and Cage thought Johnny should try acting. Cage helped Johnny get an agent, and in 1987 Johnny got a part on the TV series 21 Jump Street. This brought him fame as a teen idol. When the TV series finished, he starred in Cry-Baby and then the wildly popular Edward Scissorhands. Roles in the hit movies Pirates of the Caribbean, Sweeney Todd, and Alice in Wonderland followed.

Today, Johnny lives with French actress Vanessa Paradis and their two children. They have houses in France, the US, and on a private Caribbean island. Johnny's hobbies include playing the guitar, reading, painting, and collecting fine French wines.

UNIT 6 Destinations

▶ 1.33 (Page 58)

1. Ninety Mile Beach
2. Tongariro mountain
3. Tasman Sea
4. South Pacific Ocean
5. Kawarau river
6. Lake Wakatipu
7. Stewart island

▶ 1.34 (Page 58)

Tour guide: New Zealand is a surprising country with a population of 4 million people and 40 million sheep. The capital city is Wellington, but the largest city is Auckland. There are two official languages—English and Maori, and the national symbol is a small bird called a kiwi.

New Zealand's tourist industry is based on outdoor sports. Go to the beautiful beaches of North Island if you like swimming, surfing, or scuba diving. South Island is the place for you if you prefer mountain walking, skiing, or bungee jumping.

There's plenty of culture, too, with, . . .

▶ **1.35** (Page 60)

M1: . . . No, I missed it. What happened?

F1: Well, three families had to live like Wild West settlers from the 1880s. They didn't have any modern things. No TV, no phone, no shampoo, very few clothes, and the nearest store was ten miles away. One family, the Clunes from California, had a very difficult time.

M1: Why? What did they find difficult?

F1: Well, Gordon, the father, did a lot of hard physical work and he lost a lot of weight. He chopped down trees and built the house when they first got there, and basically he worked very hard all the time.

M1: What about the mother?

F1: She had a hard time, too. She couldn't stand wearing the same clothes every day, and she hated not wearing make-up. She had to cook, clean the house, wash clothes, etc., all without any machines. And they were always hungry.

M1: Did the children enjoy it?

F1: At first, they complained that there was too much to do. They had to help with the animals, cooking, chopping wood, etc. The teenage girls missed shopping and their friends, and the younger boys missed the TV and skateboarding.

M1: Did they change over the six months?

F1: Yes. They all changed. Near the end of the 6 months, Tracy, who was 15, said she didn't care about make-up and clothes . . . what is important is being with your family and friends and really getting to know them. I think they all felt the same.

M1: So what happened when they went home to their modern life?

F1: Well, back home in California . . .

▶ **1.36** (Page 60)

M1: So what happened when they went home to their modern life?

F1: Well, back in California, they loved seeing their friends again and wearing different clothes and stuff. But the children, especially the teenagers, were really bored.

M1: Bored?

F1: Yes. I think they realized that there is more to life than make-up, TV, and clothes! They really missed having all the jobs to do. They missed the fresh air and the time spent with their families.

▶ **1.37** (Page 61)

M1: OK, so we have to choose five machines we can't live without.

F1: Yup.

M1: And we're going to live in the Wild West for six months.

F1: Yes . . .

M1: As now or as a hundred years ago?

F1: As they did a hundred years ago.

M1: OK, how about I start?

F1: Go ahead.

M1: Well, we could live without a cell phone, but I'd like to choose a TV, because I couldn't live without a TV for six months!

F1: Oh, no. Not a TV! I think people watch too much TV, and anyway, we'll be too busy. I think we should take a radio.

M1: A radio? Why's that?

F1: Well, the main reason is that we can listen to music while we work—and you have to work hard in the Wild West. I always listen to the radio while I'm cleaning or cooking.

M1: OK. Good point. What else? . . . Um . . . how about a washing machine, because I'm too lazy to wash clothes by hand.

F1: Yes, I agree. OK, so that's two things. What else?

M1: I'd also like to take a . . . DVD player.

F1: You're joking, aren't you! We're not taking a TV, so how can we watch DVDs?

M1: Good point. Well . . .

▶ **1.39** (Page 65)

M1: Well, what do you think? We're going in March so we need to get the tickets soon. Where would you like to go?

F1: I think Barcelona sounds really good or maybe Beijing . . . I'm not sure. There are lots of great things to see and do in both places. What do you think?

M1: Um . . . I think Beijing is too cold for a vacation . . . I like warmer weather . . . 43° is too cold! Barcelona is a little bit warmer. Is it warm enough?

F1: Yes, I think so . . . It's warm enough for me . . .

M1: But look . . . Hotels in Barcelona are expensive . . . $160 a night.

F1: That's not too expensive. We can afford that. Let's go to Barcelona!

M1: OK . . . What's it like in Barcelona? Are there lots of interesting things to do?

F1: I'm sure there are. Let's check the guidebook.

UNIT 7 Mind and body

▶ **2.02** (Page 69)

M1: Well, I think this person is very good-looking. He or she is tall and slightly overweight—well, not overweight, but big—and pretty muscular. Guess who?

F1: OK, this person is . . . very skinny actually. He or she isn't short . . . In fact, I'd say this person is slightly taller than average. And he or she is a lot more attractive than most. Guess who . . . ?

▶ **2.03** (Page 69)

M1: Don't be shy! Admit it! Men want to look after their skin as much as women do. How will you feel if you look in the mirror tomorrow morning? Will you feel happy with what you see? Or will you see that your face needs serious help?

Don't worry! Help is here! New Face Saver face cream from New Man Cosmetics will save your skin from all the problems of modern living. If you use Face Saver once a day, you'll soon have softer, fresher skin. And you'll certainly notice the difference if you use Face Saver twice a day. Use it morning and evening to look years younger.

Don't waste another day! Use Face Saver from New Man Cosmetics, and save your skin before it's too late!

▶ **2.05** (Page 72)

F1: Hey, listen to these jokes! I think they're really funny.

M1: Let's hear 'em.

F1: "Doctor, doctor, I've lost my memory."

"When did this happen?"

"When did what happen?"

M1: That's pretty funny.

F1: What about this one? "Doctor, doctor, I get a pain in my eye when I drink coffee."

"Have you tried taking the spoon out?"

M1: . . . I don't get it. Taking the spoon out? . . . Oh! I see. Oh yeah, I get it.

F1: OK. This is a good one. "Doctor, doctor, when I press my finger on my stomach it hurts. Do I have food poisoning?"

"No, you have a broken finger."

M1: Hah . . . That's very good.

▶ **2.06** (Page 72)

Illnesses

F1: I have the flu.

F1: I have a cold.

F1: I have food poisoning.

Injuries

M1: I have a broken arm.

M1: I have a broken leg.

Symptoms

F1: I have a headache.

F1: I have a sore throat.

F1: I have an earache.

F1: I have a pain in my chest.

F1: I have a stomach ache.

F1: I feel sick.

F1: I have a fever.

F1: I have a toothache.

F1: I have a backache.

UNIT 8 Life in the fast lane

▶ **2.08** (Page 79)

1. The number of fast-food restaurants is going up steadily.
2. The quality of food that most people eat has gotten worse recently.
3. The amount of traffic has increased over the last few years.
4. The air quality in most cities is deteriorating rapidly.

▶ **2.09** (Page 81)

1

F1: Hi . . . my name's Melanie. What's your name?

M1: I'm Steve—nice to meet you. What do you do, Melanie?

F1: Oh, I'm a teacher. And you?

M1: I'm an architect.

F1: Oh, that's interesting. Do you enjoy your job?

M1: Yes, I do. It's . . . very interesting. Um, do you know much about architecture?

F1: No, not really.

M1: Oh. Have you done speed-dating before?

F1: No. This is my first time. How about you?

M1: Well actually, this is my third time, but I haven't had much luck yet . . .

2

F2: Hello. I'm Rachel.

M2: Hi Rachel. My name's Kieron.

F2: OK, we've only got three minutes so . . . how would your best friend describe you?

M2: Well . . . I think my best friend would say I'm friendly and open, and that I love traveling.

F2: Traveling? So what's the most amazing place that you've travelled to?

M2: Oh, Canada, definitely. It's just so beautiful. Tell me something about you. What was the last CD you bought?

F2: Well actually, it was a teach-yourself-Italian CD. I'm learning Italian.

M2: That's a coincidence, because I'm learning Italian, too!

F2: Really? Why are you learning it?

M2: Well, I really love the country, and I want to be able to speak the language when I'm there . . .

UNIT 9 Careers

▶ **2.11** (Page 92)

Newscaster: . . . and in local news, a very unusual car thief was sentenced to ten years in jail today. The thief, Los Angeles factory worker Dave Grumbel, was charged with stealing 39 luxury cars. The cars, worth close to $4 million in all, were stolen from dealerships all over California. The court was told that Grumbel repeatedly visited car dealerships and, after befriending the sales staff, would ask to test drive a car. He never returned the cars. Instead, he sprayed the cars with expensive perfume and then drove them for several days. Each of the cars was later found along the side of Highway One. He was called "the Chanel Number Five" thief by the media.

In interviews, Mr. Grumbel explained his actions. He said it made him feel rich to drive nice, new cars. He said he liked to pretend he was wealthy and had as many cars as he wanted. Grumbel was caught when he was seen leaving one of the stolen cars on Highway One. A police officer smelled the inside of the car, and knew he had the "Chanel" thief.

▶ **2.12** (Page 95)

M1: Morning, Laura . . . or should I say "Afternoon"?

F1: Ha ha . . . . can you pass me the cereal Dad?

M1: So, what are you doing today?

F1: Oh nothing . . . going out . . .

M1: Fine, but make sure you clean your room before you do. It's a complete mess.

F1: Well, it's none of your business. It's my room.

M1: Yes, well, this is my house . . . and while you live in it, you do what I say. Got it?

F1: Yeah right.

UNIT 10 Animal planet

▶ **2.13** (Page 99)

1. Where did you grow up?
2. Who brought you up?
3. As a child, who looked after you when you were ill?
4. As a child, who did you look up to?
5. Have you ever picked up any English from TV or songs?
6. Have you ever come across any money in the street?

▶ **2.14** (Page 99)

F1: Well . . . I guess I had a bit of an odd childhood. I mean, it was pretty different from all my friends. My parents separated when I was really young—I was about three, I think. They stayed friends, so I saw my dad every so often. That was fine . . . but it was my mom who really brought me up. You see, she taught English, and we lived overseas a lot. In fact, she spent a long time in Tokyo, Japan—that's where I was born and pretty much where I grew up. I've always been incredibly close to my mom . . . and also to my grandmother. I really look up to my grandmother. She's a wonderful person. I mean, she's very kind and generous. We all get along really well . . . of course, we have the occasional fight but . . . that's normal I think. So, anyway, I came back to the States when I was a teenager and went to school . . . but I didn't really like any of my teachers. School wasn't easy for me.

▶ **2.15** (Page 102)

Welcome to Pet News. Want to stay in a luxury resort with your dog? Inn by the Sea in Crescent Beach, Maine, might be the answer. Located on beautiful Crescent Beach, the Inn has welcomed dogs for over 15 years. The Inn offers a free water bowl, beach towels, blankets, and treats for all dog guests. The Inn also provides owners with a list of nearby walking trails, dog-friendly beaches, and parks. In addition to the standard service, the Inn offers a special Inncredible Pet package for you and your dog. The package includes two nights in a suite. When you arrive, your dog gets a welcome toy and his own dog bed, personalized with his name. And every night, your dog can select dinner from the gourmet doggy menu, designed to appeal to the pickiest eater. Main dishes include "the bird dog," with grilled chicken, rice, and vegetables, and "doggy gumbo,"

with Angus beef, rice, and vegetables. All main courses come with a dog cookie. In addition to dinner, the Inncredible Pet package includes a locally made dog treat delivered to your room at bedtime. During your stay, your pampered dog will also receive a 30-minute in-room massage. The Inncredible Pet package starts at $307 per night.

UNIT 11 World travel

▶ **2.17** (Page 108)

F1: Andy, um . . . we need to talk . . .

M1: Sure, what's up?

F1: Well, I was thinking . . . I think we need to travel separately now . . .

M1: Oh! Really? I'm having a lot of fun traveling with you . . .

F1: Well . . . yeah . . . I like traveling with you too . . . but . . . I want to practice my Portuguese, and when I'm with you, we just speak English all the time . . .

M1: Oh—well, I promise I'll speak Portuguese to you.

F1: No . . . I don't really think that would work, do you?

M1: No . . . you're probably right . . .

▶ **2.18** (Page 109)

M or F: So, you want to find your perfect travel companion . . . First, answer these questions . . .
1. Do you like very hot places?
2. Do you like talkative travel companions?
3. Which activity do you like best: sightseeing, hanging out at the beach, skiing, or camping?
4. Do you like staying in hotels or renting apartments?
5. Do you like to go out a lot at night?
6. Do you like trying food from other countries?

▶ **2.19** (Page 112)

M1: It's great to have you with us today. So . . . how did you start traveling?

F1: Well, as a child, I traveled a lot with my family. We went on some fantastic trips, like biking through Europe when I was 13. By the time I was 16, I had visited 19 countries!

M1: Wow. And how did you start writing?

F1: Well, when I traveled I always kept a diary. I didn't want to forget all the things that I had seen and experienced. So I wrote it all down. At first, it was just facts. Then I added my feelings and stories about the places and the people.

M1: It's sometimes difficult to get started as a writer . . . What was your first "break" as a travel writer?

F1: It was luck, really. I had lived in Korea for about two years. Then a friend of mine, who worked for a travel agency, said he needed someone to write a travel guide about Korea. So I did it! Other writing jobs came from that.

M1: And what is the most difficult thing when you are traveling?

F1: The language can be difficult. I love talking to people. But sometimes it's hard work when you can't speak the language.

M1: That makes sense. And what is the most difficult thing when you are writing?

F1: When I get home from traveling, I have notebooks full of notes. I often feel like writing about everything. The most difficult thing is deciding what to include and what to leave out.

M1: Mm-hmm. Which travel authors or books have influenced you?

F1: It was Paul Theroux who made me really want to be a travel writer. His books are so interesting and really funny.

M1: What advice would you give to someone thinking of being a travel writer?

F1: First, read as many books as you can. And second, take notes of as many details as you can when you're traveling. Finally, go for it! Being a travel writer really is a dream job!

▶ **2.21** (Page 112)

1. By the time I was 16, I had visited 19 countries.
2. I hadn't been there very long when I got the job.
3. Had you written any other books before this one was published?

▶ **2.22** (Page 113)

1. By the time I arrived at the station, the train had left.
2. When we got there, we realized we hadn't packed enough warm clothes.
3. I decided to go back to the same place I had gone on my last vacation.
4. As soon as I saw Carolina, I realized I had met her before.

▶ **2.23** (Page 115)

F1: Hi. Can I help you?

M1: Yes, I'd like a ticket to Scarsdale, please.

F1: One-way or round-trip?

M1: Round-trip, please.

F1: That'll be $16.

M1: Can I pay by debit card?

F1: Yes, just swipe your card there and enter your PIN.

M1: Oh, OK. And when is the next train?

F1: The next train is at 8:24.

M1: What track will it be on?

F1: It'll be on track 21.

M1: Twenty-one. And what time does it get into Scarsdale?

F1: It arrives in Scarsdale at . . . 9:06.

M1: Great, thanks.

F1: Here's your ticket. Have a nice day.

UNIT 12 Money matters

▶ **2.24** (Page 120)

M1: . . . and finally . . . A high school in Chicago has given $20,000 to its seniors for getting good test results. Before students took their final exams, the school gave each student target grades to try and achieve. Now that the results of the tests are in, Hamilton High School has given $50 to students who achieved their target grades and an additional $500 to every student who got into college.

"The results this year show the success of the program," said Marisa Ortega, vice principal. "Unlike a lot of programs, this one rewards every student for doing well, not just the best students."

I asked people what they thought of the program. First, I spoke to a parent of a student at the school and asked her how she felt about rewarding students with money.

F1: Well . . . I'm not really sure. It feels a little bit like bribery to me. I mean, young people should study hard for tests because they want to do well and get a good education. Not because they'll earn some money!

M1: Later I spoke to David Lee, a history teacher at Hamilton. He was delighted with the program and told me that more students had gotten into college this year than ever before.

Kelly, a student at Hamilton, said she had earned over $500 and was really pleased. She also said that she thought it was a great idea . . . and that it'd made her work much harder. When I asked what she was going to do with the money, she said she was going to buy a new computer.

So, a controversial approach, but one that seems to work for some students! And now . . . over to Alex for the weather . . .

▶ **2.26** (Page 123)

1. Neither of my two best friends is married yet.
2. Both of my parents have always worked.
3. Neither of them is retired yet.
4. Let's see either a movie or a play.
5. I prefer a play, but either is OK with me.

▶ **2.27** (Page 125)

1

F1: Excuse me, I think there's a mistake with the bill.

M1: Oh really?

F1: We actually had only two coffees, not three.

M1: Oh yes, you're right. I'm very sorry ma'am, I'll take it off the bill.

2

M2: Hello, I'd like to speak to someone about this sweater. I bought it a couple of weeks ago.

F2: Sure . . . what seems to be the problem?

M2: Well, the first time I washed it the color came out and turned all my other clothes pink . . . AND . . . it shrank . . . I mean, now look at it. It wouldn't fit a child.

F2: Oh yes, I see what you mean . . . Can I ask what temperature you washed it at?

M2: Just a normal wash . . . I think it's just poor quality. I'd like a refund, please.

3

M3: Here's your book . . . and . . . your change.

F3: I'm sorry but I gave you a $20 bill. I should have $14.60 in change, not $4.60.

M3: Whoops, you're right. Here's the correct change. I don't know what I was thinking about.